Passing the Police Recruit Assessment Process

Second edition

Passing the Police Recruit Assessment Process

Second edition

PETER COX

LearningMatters

First published in 2007 by Law Matters Ltd.

Reprinted in 2007.
Reprinted in 2008 (twice).
Reprinted in 2009.

Second edition published in 2010 by Learning Matters Ltd.

British Library Cataloguing in Publication Data
A CIP record for this book is available from the British Library.

ISBN: 978 1 84445 358 0

This book is also available in the following ebook formats:
Adobe ebook ISBN: 978 1 84445 669 7
EPUB ebook ISBN: 978 1 84445 668 0
Kindle ISBN: 978 1 84445 975 9

Cover design by Code 5 Design Associates Ltd
Project management by Deer Park Productions, Tavistock
Typeset by Pantek Arts Ltd, Maidstone, Kent
Printed and bound in Great Britain by Bell & Bain Ltd, Glasgow

Learning Matters Ltd
33 Southernhay East
Exeter EX1 1NX
Tel: 01392 215560
info@learningmatters.co.uk
www.learningmatters.co.uk

Mixed Sources
Product group from well-managed
forests and other controlled sources
www.fsc.org Cert no. TT-COC-002769
© 1996 Forest Stewardship Council

Contents

Acknowledgements

Peter Cox would like to thank his wife Janice for all the support, help and encouragement she gave him during his police career and while writing this book.

Every effort has been made to trace the copyright holders and to obtain their permission for the use of copyright material. The publisher and author will gladly receive information enabling them to rectify any error or omission in subsequent editions.

The author and publisher would like to thank the following for permission to reproduce copyright material:

The Integrated Competency Behavioural Framework – Version 9.0 (May 2007) reproduced, in part, in Appendix A of this book with the kind permission of Skills for Justice.

Chapter 1

Introduction

Why this book?

The National Police Recruit Assessment Process operates at the highest standards possible, but the advice and guidance available to people who are considering undergoing this assessment process are limited and vary in quality. This book, therefore, includes not only an explanation of the National Police Recruit Assessment Process but also exercises that have been designed to help you acquire or enhance the skills and abilities you need to become a police officer.

You should work through the contents of this book in the order they are presented. This will assist you in understanding:

- whether a career in the police service is for you;
- the reasons why a National Police Recruit Assessment Process has been established;
- the National Core Competencies;
- how to complete the written application;
- what is included in the assessment;
- the requirements for each section of the assessment;
- the skills and abilities required to be a police officer (these are tested during the assessment process); and
- the feedback you receive following an assessment.

You should create a self-study plan when using this book. How you devise this and the detail it contains will be dictated by the time you have available prior to attending for your assessment.

When you are preparing for the assessment process, you must obtain certain information and guidance. This will help you when you come to consider and develop your skills and abilities. It is important that you obtain information and guidance from more than one person: detailed feedback from a number of different sources will enable you to assess yourself accurately and will help you to develop the appropriate skills. Try, therefore, to get help from at least three different people, preferably from different walks of life (for example, from your family, work and social environments). You should also read – and make sure you understand – the information you receive from the Police Service to which you have applied. This should be received at least two weeks before you attend for assessment.

A number of issues are mentioned on more than one occasion in this book. This will help you to understand the requirements for that particular part of the assessment process and will also reinforce the key learning points.

Is a career in the police service for you?

A career in the police has been portrayed in endless television programmes, usually in a positive way showing the more enjoyable and rewarding aspects of being a police officer. Within the longer-running police series people can often move from routine uniform duties to specialised units as well as getting promoted. Before making an application to be a police officer it is often worth considering the parts of the service that are not usually demonstrated within the shows.

Police officers obviously work across 24 hours a day seven days a week. People joining as a constable always know this but the practical realities often only strike after they become operational. Over the years each police service has attempted to align their resources to meet the demands for help and assistance from the public. These demands are usually far fewer between 9 a.m. and 5 p.m., Monday to Friday when most people are at work, in education or are out and about shopping. For most police areas this means having the minimum numbers of staff on duty during these periods. This allows the maximum number of officers to be available during other times. In real terms this means a great deal of evening and weekend work. Any potential officer needs to consider whether working hours to fit public requirements will fit in with their own and their family's lifestyle. It is not for everyone.

While the hours can be demanding it must also be remembered that bank holidays and days off around them can often be very limited. Just consider a New Year's Eve. The biggest numbers of officers possible will be required during the evening and early hours of New Year's Day. Major sporting events and demonstrations also require much policing. Even when events are not within this country they can have a dramatic effect on policing requirements. When the England football team competes in World Cup finals, on the days they play there are often increased demands on police to attend public order disturbances after the games have finished, particularly if England has been eliminated. It is not unusual to have rest days cancelled for such events, often affecting personal plans that individual officers have made.

Television programmes never show the amount of writing that has to be completed by officers across a wide range of duties and activities. If this were shown, no doubt viewing figures would plummet. It is often said that a police officer is only as good as their ability to write about what they saw and heard, what they did and why they did it. Making the best arrest in the world is not a lot of use if the subsequent court file is not presented appropriately or does not have sufficient evidence to secure a conviction. Any police officer will tell you that writing is a major part of their job.

Dealing with conflict, whether aimed at officers directly or at other members of the public, can be a major part of a constable's role, often ending up in both verbal and physical assaults on officers. Thankfully the majority of such attacks are minor but they can become routine to officers who regularly deal with public order offences. Being able to deal with conflict is a must for all officers. If you really shy away from conflict or find it really challenging then a career in the police service is probably not for you.

Over recent decades civilian police employees have replaced more and more job roles that were traditionally completed by police officers; for example, the looking after of prisoners held within police custody. Even activities such as interviewing suspects can be completed by civilians with specialist skills. While many specialist roles are no longer available to officers, others have developed; however, it must be remembered that as a minimum most officers will spend at least their first two years on uniformed duties dealing with day-to-day routine policing activities.

Any job will have down sides but a police career can be rewarding in both financial terms and personal satisfaction. Members of the public can be very grateful for the actions of police officers often in the most trying of circumstances. It can still provide opportunities for promotion or to specialise. It can be exciting and provides training that allows for development of skills and abilities that can be used not only in the service but also throughout life in general.

Before applying, any potential officer should consider what they want from a career, what they enjoy and the lifestyle they wish to have. They should then decide whether that is compatible with the role of being a police constable.

What do recruiters to the police service look for?

Recruiters to the police service have always looked for individuals who have firstly considered for themselves the demanding requirements that the role of constable would place on them. Having done that then decide that they still want to face those challenges and have the appropriate skills to be able to do so.

In previous generations the actual skills that recruiters were looking for were often not well defined and could vary from police service to police service. The recruit assessment process has changed that and now both the recruiters and candidates can be very clear as to the skills that are required to be an effective constable. It is these skills that are looked for during the recruit process.

Background to the National Police Recruit Assessment Process

Before the National Police Recruit Assessment Process was established, each police service in England and Wales was responsible for its own recruiting methods. This led to variations in the skills and abilities that were being assessed, and to what standards. In addition, the actual assessment of individual candidates varied a great deal. It was for these reasons that a nationally recognised, robust and standardised procedure was proposed. The result was the National Police Recruit Assessment Process, which was designed and implemented by the national police training organisation, Centrex, now known as NPIA.

As part of this process, 'Assessment Centres' were created. Even though the term 'Assessment Centre' suggests otherwise, an Assessment Centre is really a process rather than a building or a place. For a recruiting process to be considered an Assessment Centre, certain key elements must be present.

- The candidates' skills and abilities are tested a number of different times.

- These skills and abilities are tested through different exercises and tests.

- The assessments that arise from these exercises and tests are used to produce the final results.

- A number of assessors are used throughout the process.

- These assessors must have the appropriate training before they are permitted to assess.

Using different exercises and tests and a number of trained assessors ensures fairness and equality for all: the candidates are given a range of opportunities to display the skills necessary to become a police officer.

If a traditional recruitment interview was used as the only method of selection, this would suit some candidates more than others. For example, if a candidate started the interview badly, it would be very difficult for him or her to recover, causing the candidate to feel that he or she was unable to show his or her real abilities. At an Assessment Centre, however, candidates move quickly from one exercise or test to the next. It is therefore important not to dwell on what has just happened but to focus on what comes next.

Approximately eight assessors contribute to the assessment of each individual candidate. These people are not given any information about the candidates they are to assess. In addition, they are unable to communicate with the other assessors before they begin their assessments. This ensures that, at each stage of the process, a candidate is starting with a clean slate as far as that assessor is concerned.

It is thus generally accepted that Assessment Centres are more reliable in recruiting appropriate people when compared with single-form recruiting methods, such as traditional interviews. It is for this reason that, within the police service, Assessment Centres are used not only for recruitment purposes but also for promotion.

Assessment Centre exercises

Each set of exercises takes approximately six months to design and develop before it reaches an appropriate standard whereby it can be used to assess candidates. This design process follows nationally agreed standards and has various phases. These include:

- research;

- design;

- development;

- trials;

- review;

- refinement.

Many exercises are discarded at different stages of the design process if they are shown to contain any weaknesses or flaws. Those that are selected must demonstrate in each phase that they will assess candidates consistently and fairly.

Those involved in the design process include occupational psychologists, people trained in recruitment processes and laypeople representing a wide cross-section of the community. In total, approximately 500 people will be involved, at some stage, in the design process.

How candidates are assessed

Clusters of skills and abilities are assessed during each exercise. These are called the National Core Competencies, which are discussed in the next chapter. At the conclusion of the assessment process, the same competency areas from each of the exercises are added together. This means that, if problem-solving is considered in four exercises, the scores for these four exercises will be added together, resulting in a total score for the area of problem-solving. In this way a candidate will not fail the entire assessment simply because he or she has performed badly in one particular exercise. Candidates are thus given every opportunity to demonstrate their skills and abilities and to achieve an assessment that reflects those skills and abilities.

There is one exception to this: the area of Respect for Race and Diversity. Should a candidate display behaviour that is totally inappropriate for the conduct of a police officer, then that candidate will be considered unsuitable, no matter how good his or her other skills and abilities are, or how well he or she performs in this competency area in other exercises. The reason for this is simple: when a police officer deals with the public, if he or she behaves badly, it does not matter how well he or she resolves the issue, the public's perception of the police is likely to be poor. This will probably remain so even if all their other interactions with the police are favourable. (The area of Respect for Race and Diversity is explained in more detail in **Chapter 8**.)

The required standard

The required standard of performance is the same for all candidates, but it is altered from time to time for a variety of reasons. It will, however, usually require the candidates to achieve a minimum of 60 per cent of the total score available to be successful. All candidates' scores are judged against a preset standard – candidates are not judged against one another.

When a candidate has completed an assessment, his or her scores for each exercise, and for each competency area, are added together. These scores are combined with the scores from the other areas to arrive at the final mark. The minimum set score must be achieved to be successful. This scoring system allows candidates to be below the set level in one particular area (such as Problem Solving) but to be above the minimum in another skills set. The set minimum, however, must be achieved in the area of Respect for Race and Diversity and in a candidate's written communications because these are considered critical to being an effective police officer.

Assessors

The assessors used at Assessment Centres come from all walks of life, including the police service. While some people say that only police officers should be allowed to assess, it can also be argued that the community in general should contribute to selecting those people who will be entrusted with enforcing law and order.

Before they are allowed to assess, the assessors must undergo training. This training includes role acting because assessors are required to role act during the interactive exercises. In addition to this initial training, prior to any Assessment Centre commencing, assessors are trained in the exercise that they will operate for the duration of that Assessment Centre. Before they begin to assess and during the time they are assessing they are tested to ensure the appropriate high standards are maintained from the beginning of the assessment right through to its conclusion.

The Assessment Centre management team

In addition to trained assessors, each Assessment Centre has a designated management team. These people have the responsibility for setting up and administrating the Assessment Centre and for ensuring that all policies, procedures and guidelines are followed correctly. Depending on the number of candidates to be assessed each day, this team usually comprises of approximately eight people.

Management team members will have been trained appropriately and they constantly monitor the exercises and tests to see that they are working correctly. This ensures that every candidate, from the first to the last, gets the same opportunity to display his or her skills and abilities.

General assumptions

Throughout the book you will find 'General assumption' boxes. These boxes contain the preconceived ideas many candidates have prior to their attending an Assessment Centre. These ideas often originate from candidates who have previously attended an Assessment Centre or from unofficial websites. Many of these assumptions are wrong, misleading or incomplete.

These boxes not only highlight what is generally assumed about Assessment Centres but also list the facts of the situation. An example is as follows.

GENERAL ASSUMPTION

If you perform very badly in one exercise you will fail the Assessment Centre.

> **FACT**
>
> This is not the case. In each exercise a number of skill areas will be assessed. These are added to the scores for the same skill areas when these areas are assessed during other exercises or tests. All the scores from each exercise are then added together. It is the overall score that is important, not the score achieved in any particular exercise. As mentioned above, the only exception to this is the area of Respect for Race and Diversity and a candidate's written communications.

If you have any preconceived ideas about Assessment Centres, it is worth checking to see if these are accurate: this book will assist you in this.

Tasks

This book contains tasks for you to consider and complete. Some have been designed to demonstrate the types of exercises you will meet during the assessment. If you familiarise yourself with the exercise types now, during your assessment you will be able to concentrate on displaying the appropriate skills and abilities rather than being concerned with the mechanics of the process.

Other tasks ask you to consider the current level of your skills and abilities against those required to be a police officer, and to consider how these can be monitored and developed before you attend for an assessment. It is important that you view these tasks as a way of gaining the skills necessary to be an efficient and effective police officer, not as tricks or as a way to pass at an Assessment Centre. The more time you devote to these tasks before you attend the Assessment Centre, the greater will be your chances of demonstrating your true skills and abilities when you do attend.

> **GENERAL ASSUMPTION**
>
> You can be trained to pass an Assessment Centre.

> **FACT**
>
> You can be trained so that you understand how the Assessment Centre operates, and this training will make you more comfortable during the process. Equally, you can be trained in the skills and abilities (called competencies) that will be tested during an assessment. To be successful, you should develop your skills and abilities rather than train in a system for passing.

Top tips

Most chapters close with a 'top tips' box. These can be used as a refresher or as a revision aid. They should help you to reinforce the key learning points for each chapter. If there is anything in a top-tips box you do not understand, reread the relevant parts of that chapter. Space has been provided after each top-tips box so that you can add your own individual learning points for referring to at a later date.

The top-tips boxes look as follows.

TOP TIPS

- Devise and follow a self-study plan.

- Use more than one source of information when preparing for the Assessment Centre.

- Always read the information you receive from the police service to which you have applied regarding the Assessment Centre.

- When completing an exercise at the Assessment Centre, do not reflect on what you have just done – concentrate on what comes next.

- Remember, you are in competition with the Assessment Centre standards, not with other candidates.

- Use the 'assumption boxes' to help you consider your own preconceived ideas.

- Look to develop skills and abilities necessary to be a police officer rather than skills and abilities to pass at the Assessment Centre.

- Use the top tips to reinforce the key learning points.

- Record any personal learning from the chapter under the heading 'Individual learning points'.

INDIVIDUAL LEARNING POINTS

_____

_____

_____

_____

_____

_____

_____

_____

_____

_____

Chapter 2
The National Core Competencies

Introduction

The National Core Competencies are a list of indicators that describe the attributes necessary, across a range of skills and abilities, to become a police officer. They simply describe the attitudes and behaviours that are required (or that should be avoided) during everyday interactions.

During the assessment, seven core competencies are assessed.

(1) Respect for Race and Diversity.

(2) Team Working.

(3) Community and Customer Focus.

(4) Effective Communication.

(5) Problem Solving.

(6) Personal Responsibility.

(7) Resilience.

Each competency area comprises of a title, a description (in sentence form) of what the area means and a further statement describing the required standard for that competency. Below each area is a list of positive and negative indicators. These describe the types of attitudes and behaviours that should, or should not, be used by police officers. (**Appendix A** contains a full list of the National Core Competencies taken from Skills for Justice *Integrated Competency Behavioural Framework – Version 9.0*, but do not read this until you have completed Task 1 in this chapter.)

When you look at the list of National Core Competencies, you will see that there are many different ways you can demonstrate these indicators during an assessment. **Chapter 5** contains a sample interactive exercise assessment checklist, and this demonstrates how behaviours are assessed and linked to the competencies. Occasionally, the words used within the headings or descriptions are amended but, if this happens, it is unlikely that the skills you are required to demonstrate during an assessment will have changed.

Which competencies are assessed in which exercises

You will not usually know which competencies are being assessed in the exercises, but each competency will be assessed a minimum of three times. Remember that Respect for Race and Diversity is assessed throughout the entire process and that your oral communication skills are assessed during all interactive exercises and during the interview.

With the exception of the interview, you should not concern yourself with which of the competencies is being assessed: focus on what is in front of you. During the interview, on the other hand, you will be told which competency area is being assessed in each question, so your answers should focus on the required abilities within that area.

Develop the required skills prior to attending for assessment and then apply those skills accordingly. Refining these skills and abilities is the key to a successful police career, as it is these skills and abilities that are monitored in annual appraisals and looked for in applications for specialist roles and promotion.

Using the competencies to prepare for an assessment

Before you attend for an assessment, you should use the positive and negative indicators to help you to prepare in the following ways.

- By identifying the key requirements for each of the competency areas.
- By reviewing your current skills against the competencies.
- By developing your positive traits.
- By ceasing or amending your negative behaviours.

Developing your skills against the competencies

A systematic way to develop your skills and abilities is to undertake the following tasks.

1 Review what competencies are required.

2 Assess your current skill levels.

3 Develop and implement action plans for those areas where you are not achieving the competency requirements and to improve your overall performance.

TASK 1

Reviewing what skills and abilities are required

Listed below are the headings for each competency area. These are followed by sentences that explain what the areas are about. Below this is a statement describing the required standard for each competency area. Finally, there are spaces in the boxes with the headings 'Positives' and 'Negatives'.

To work out what skills and abilities are required to be a police officer, read each competency heading, the sentence that explains what the area is about and the statement outlining the required standard.

In the positive boxes, list what you believe would be the skills and abilities required for that competency area. Similarly, list what you believe would be the negative traits. To assist you with this, a few example traits have been given for the area of Respect for Race and Diversity. You should try to record approximately ten traits for each area.

Respect for Race and Diversity
A police officer:
Considers and shows respect for the opinions, circumstances and feelings of colleagues and members of the public, no matter what their race, religion, position, background, circumstances, status or appearance.

Required standard
A police officer:
Understands other people's views and takes them into account.
Is tactful and diplomatic when dealing with people.
Treats people with dignity and respect at all times.
Understands, and is sensitive to, social, cultural and racial differences.

Positives	*Negatives*
Understanding other people's views	*Not taking into account other people's needs*
Speaking correctly to the public	*Using offensive language*
Not breaking confidences	*Telling inappropriate jokes*

TASK 1

Team Working
A police officer:
Develops strong working relationships inside and outside the team to achieve common goals.
Breaks down barriers between groups and involves others in discussion and decisions.

Required standard
A police officer:
Works effectively as a team member and helps build relationships within the team.
Actively helps and supports others to achieve team goals.

Positives	*Negatives*

Community and Customer Focus
A police officer:
Focuses on the customer and provides a high-quality service that is tailored to meet their individual needs.
Understands the communities that are served and shows an active commitment to policing that reflects their needs and concerns.

Required standard
A police officer:
Provides a high level of service to customers.
Maintains contact with customers, works out what they need and responds to them.

Positives	*Negatives*

TASK 1

Effective Communication

A police officer:

Communicates ideas and information effectively, both verbally and in writing.

Uses language and a style of communication that are appropriate to the situation and people being addressed.

Makes sure that others understand what is going on.

Required standard

A police officer:

Communicates all needs, instructions and decisions clearly.

Adapts the style of communication to meet the needs of the audience.

Checks for understanding.

Positives	*Negatives*

Problem Solving

A police officer:

Gathers information from a range of sources.

Analyses information to identify problems and issues and makes effective decisions.

Required standard

A police officer:

Gathers enough relevant information to understand specific issues and events.

Uses information to identify problems and draws logical conclusions.

Makes good decisions.

Positives	*Negatives*

TASK 1

Personal Responsibility
A police officer:
Takes personal responsibility for making things happen and achieving results.
Displays motivation, commitment, perseverance and conscientiousness.
Acts with a high degree of integrity.

Required standard
A police officer:
Takes personal responsibility for own actions and for sorting out issues or problems that arise.
Is focused on achieving results to required standards and developing skills and knowledge.

Positives	*Negatives*

Resilience
A police officer:
Shows resilience, even in difficult circumstances.
Is prepared to make difficult decisions and has the confidence to see them through.

Required standard
A police officer:
Shows reliability and resilience in difficult circumstances.
Remains calm and confident and responds logically and decisively in difficult situations.

Positives	*Negatives*

TASK 1

When you have done this for each competency, compare your list with the National Core Competencies in **Appendix A**. Remember to read the positive and negative indicators in the context of the descriptive sentence and the outline of the required standard.

The words you will have used may not be the same as those listed in the National Core Competencies. When making the comparison, however, what is important is the meaning rather than the specific words. You should make a note of where you have missed a behaviour or attitude, or where you have considered something as positive when it should be assessed as negative, and vice versa.

Highlight the discrepancies between your own and the national list. This will develop your understanding of each competency area and of the skills and abilities contained within it. Reread the competencies a number of times and on different occasions to make sure you understand them.

GENERAL ASSUMPTION

The competency area Respect for Race and Diversity applies only to issues of sexuality and race.

FACT

Respect for Race and Diversity does indeed relate to these issues, and they are important in modern policing, but they apply equally well to all differences in society. These differences are many and varied and may not always be immediately obvious.

For example, a group of youths aged between 10 and 14 years are playing outside a retired persons' complex to the annoyance of the residents. The difference is the age range of the two groups, and this difference may affect each group's understanding of the situation. A key element of policing is to appreciate that different groups of people have different understandings of what is going on and why it is going on. Dealing with contrasting views – without taking sides – requires understanding and sensitivity.

During the assessment you should demonstrate that you have considered and understand both viewpoints before deciding on a course of action. It is important that you base your decisions on facts and not on assumptions. Do not, for instance, assume that the youths must be in the wrong.

TASK 2

Assessing your skills against the requirements

Once you understand each of the competency areas, you should consider your current skills level within each. Take time to reflect on your skills and abilities and compare these honestly with the national standards. Use the competencies listed in **Appendix B** to record an outline of your own abilities. Each area in **Appendix B** has been separated into strengths and areas for development.

Avoid generalisations and try to be as specific as possible: think about the way you behave and speak and the attitudes you display. If it helps, consider specific incidents you have been involved in and how you assisted in resolving them. Another way to do this is to monitor yourself, noting any common themes in your behaviour or actions.

An example of how you could complete **Appendix B** is given below:

Effective Communication
Strengths *I listen to what I am being told* *I check what I have been told by asking questions* *I use different words to take into account the different people I'm speaking to (i.e. children)* *Areas for development* *I am sometimes nervous when speaking to people I do not know* *I say things without thinking through the consequences* *I can ramble when talking*

When you have completed the task, compare your strengths and areas for development with those listed in **Appendix A**. Make sure you listed things under the correct headings. For example, the following may have been listed as a strength: 'To reinforce my speech, I talk over other people to make sure I'm heard.' You may think this falls under a positive heading (i.e. 'Speaks with authority'). However, 'Does not listen' is a negative attribute. Talking over people would clearly fit into this category.

Having reflected on and recorded your own level of performance, confirm your results by obtaining feedback from family, friends or work colleagues. Select people you believe can make the most accurate judgements about you. Although it is tempting to choose only those people who, you believe, will give you positive feedback, this will not assist you in identifying areas for development.

Use the seven competency headings to help these people focus on your different skills and abilities. This will give direction to their feedback. You could also look at any appraisals you may have had in your current employment. If you do this, however, you should make sure that what is considered positive or negative in your current work would also be regarded so within a policing environment.

When you seek feedback from people, ask them to be honest and open. Should the feedback be unclear, ask them to expand their thoughts and to give precise examples where possible. This will help to confirm that the feedback is appropriate and will therefore assist you in your understanding.

For example, a friend says to you: 'Sometimes you are a bit unclear.' Try to establish exactly what he or she means.

- Do you mumble?

- Are your sentences sometimes confused?

- On occasions, do you change the direction of a conversation mid-sentence?

- Or do you use wrong or inappropriate words?

The clearer the feedback, the easier it is to work out how you can change your behaviour. Ask these people to give you examples of what you said and did. Even though it is difficult to listen to adverse comments about yourself, avoid becoming defensive and accept what you are being told. Try to decide how accurate the feedback is: compare it with your own assessment of yourself and with that of others. Come to terms with the fact that other people's perceptions of your behaviour may not be the same as your own.

At times feedback from different sources will contradict. Look for common themes that accord with your own evaluation of your abilities. In this way you should identify appropriate areas and clear targets for development.

TASK 3

Action planning to improve your performance

Having completed an evaluation of your skills and abilities and having obtained feedback from others, you should now have a clear understanding of what you do well. Continue to develop these positive skills and abilities so that your confidence increases.

You should also have gained an insight into those attitudes and abilities that require development. It's a good idea to list these to make them clear. When you have done this, grade each item in order of priority, starting with the area that received the most negative feedback.

You should now devise an action plan for each item on the list. An action plan is simply a written set of instructions to help you focus on what it is you need to do or improve, what you need to achieve and a time frame in which to do it.

Action plans

Police officers are often given developmental action plans during their training, and these usually contain the following words.

- 'Specific': an outline of those *specific* things that need to be developed or improved. This should be listed as a positive attitude or behaviour, not a negative one. For example, you realise you must allow others to stop speaking before you reply, rather than talking over them. This section of the plan should contain an outline of how you are to go about this, perhaps in the form of simple steps you intend to take to achieve the required development.

- 'Measurable': the ways the improvement or development can be *measured*.

- 'Relevant' and 'achievable': the actions you intend to take are *relevant* in that they will actually *achieve* the required development. The action plan may not contain these words, but they will help you to consider whether the steps you are taking will bring about the required learning.

- 'Timescale': the *timescale* within which the required development can be achieved and measured should be realistic.

Obviously, the time you have available prior to attending an Assessment Centre will dictate the number and depth of any action plans you devise.

Below is an example of an action plan for a candidate who has identified that he or she often interrupts others without good reason.

Example action plan

Specific: you must allow others to finish speaking before you reply. This will be achieved by completing the following actions.

- Identifying those who can assist you with this action plan.

- Informing those people of your proposed plan and seeking their agreement to assist you in this.

- Asking them to inform you when you fail to allow others to finish speaking.

- Asking them, when appropriate, to stop you when you begin to talk before others have finished.

- Agreeing how and when they will give you feedback.

- Continuing to receive feedback until you can demonstrate that the action plan has been achieved.

Measurable: ask family, friends and work colleagues to note down when you interrupt others. Ask them to continue with this feedback even when you no longer talk over others (i.e. their feedback will be a measure of your success in your action plan).

Achievable: for your plan to be considered successful, under normal circumstances, in the majority of occasions you allow others to finish speaking before you reply.

Timescale: you will be monitored over a two-week period, during which time the circumstances and occasions when this happens will be identified. At the end of this period, you should be able to assess whether or not the action plan has been successful. If it has, no further plans for this developmental area are required, other than ongoing monitoring. For more complex plans, a timescale should be set for each individual action.

The number of action plans to be used

For each developmental area you have identified, write an action plan. It is, however, advisable to use no more than three at any one time. If you use more than three, the feedback you receive from others and your own self-monitoring may become generalised or unclear.

When you have completed an action plan, introduce a new one until all your developmental areas have been covered. However, continue to monitor your developmental areas even after an action plan has been completed – this should prevent old patterns of behaviour from returning.

TOP TIPS

- Identify each of the National Core Competencies areas.
- Identify appropriate positive and negative traits for each area.
- Identify and correct any misunderstandings regarding the competency requirements.
- Review your personal strengths and development areas against the National Core Competencies.
- Ask for feedback from family, friends and work colleagues.
- Using the National Core Competencies, identify your own personal development areas.
- Create action plans for your developmental needs.
- Prioritise your action plans.
- Activate your action plans in order of priority.
- Remember that the competency area Respect for Race and Diversity is assessed throughout the entire process.

INDIVIDUAL LEARNING POINTS

_____

_____

_____

_____

_____

_____

_____

_____

_____

Chapter 3
The Application Form

Introduction

(*Note*: If possible, have a copy of the application form next to you when reading this chapter.)

Before you can attend an Assessment Centre, you must fill in an application form and submit this to the police force of your choice. This application form has four sections.

(a) Information about yourself.

(b) Your employment history.

(c) Your education and skills.

(d) A competency assessment.

First of all, read the guidance notes on the application form before you answer any of the questions. Then, *using a piece of scrap paper*, write down exactly what you intend to put on the form, particularly in the competency assessment section. Now ask someone to read what you have written and, if necessary, to correct your spelling and grammar – you do not want your application to be rejected simply because it contains spelling and grammatical mistakes.

When you are happy with the wording, make a few photocopies of the form – again, *before* you fill it in. You can then use these copies to practise filling in the actual form. This should prevent you from making mistakes. In the competency assessment section, for example, there is only a limited amount of space for you to write your evidence. Practise filling this in: you want to provide clear evidence but not cram so many words into the box that your writing becomes illegible.

Look at the information provided at the start of each section on the form. This states clearly that, if you are not completing the form online, you should complete it in black ink. Make sure you do, and make sure the pen you intend to use has sufficient ink to fill in the entire form – a change of pen halfway through an application form looks unsightly.

Section 1: About you

All applicants are vetted to make sure they are suitable to join the police service. It is for this reason that you should complete the section regarding convictions and cautions openly and honestly. Declare all your convictions and cautions and any that may be pending – even those for motoring offences. The force you have applied to will check your form with various police databases. If you have omitted something, this will result in your application being rejected. If you are uncertain as to whether a certain conviction may bar you from applying, contact the force's recruiting department for clarification. After all, you do not want to waste your time and effort completing the application form only to find out you are ineligible.

Similar inquiries will be made about your close family and associates, and this is why it is essential you complete the section 'About your family' accurately.

As well as requirements around previous convictions the following will also be considered.

Age – Applications can be made from the age of 18. It would be expected that recruits join with the intent of at least completing the probationary period of two years before compulsory retirement, which is at the age of 60.

Nationality requirements – It is required that an applicant is a British citizen, EC/EEA national or Commonwealth citizen. You can also be a foreign national provided you have no restrictions on your stay in the United Kingdom.

Tattoos – Tattoos are not acceptable if they are thought to be garish or offensive, or could undermine the dignity and authority of the role of constable. They would also not be considered appropriate if they were in a particularly prominent area of the body, for example words or a picture across the forehead.

Financial status – Applicants will have their financial status checked. This is simply because officers can have access to very priviledged and sensitive information which can lead to individuals becoming vulnerable to corruption. Applicants should not have been registered as bankrupt with outstanding debts or have outstanding county court judgements.

Eyesight – These requirements are quite technical and reasonable sight is required for appointment; however, this can be achieved through wearing spectacles, contact lenses or corrective surgery.

Health – This, like the eyesight requirements, can be quite technical. No one can be automatically excluded on the grounds of a medical condition or disability. The requirements are in line with the Disability Discrimination Act. In general terms applicants are expected to be in good physical and mental health within the day-to-day requirements of being an effective police officer. Each individual case is considered on its merit. For example, if an applicant couldn't achieve the hearing standard, if they wished consideration could be given to their abilities with the use of a hearing aid. Such circumstances would require further investigation and consideration on a personal basis.

Previous applications – Applicants are only allowed to apply to one police service at any time. If an application is unsuccessful another cannot be made for a period of six months.

Section 2: About your employment

As with the other sections, make sure you leave yourself sufficient space to provide all the information requested. For example, the column headed 'Reason for leaving/wanting to leave' does not allow you much room for your answer. Practise filling this in on one of your photocopies. In the section about your previous employment, start with your most recent job. If you run out of space to list all your previous employment, continue on a separate sheet.

In the section headed 'Referees', ideally you should put your current or previous employer. If you have never been employed, you can provide personal references (for example, if you have been involved in voluntary work). If you are a member of Her Majesty's armed forces, you will need to provide a covering letter outlining the date or projected date of your discharge.

Section 3: About your education and skills

You do not need any formal educational qualifications, specific skills or particular experiences to apply to be a police officer. When completing this section, again, start with your most recent qualifications and work backwards. Do not cram all the details into the limited space provided: you are allowed to continue on a separate sheet.

Section 4: Competency assessment

This is the most important part of the form because you will be assessed against the information you provide. You will not progress to the next stage of the selection process if you do not provide evidence of your competency in this section.

As a reminder, the National Core Competencies are as follows.

- Respect for Race and Diversity.
- Team Working.
- Community and Customer Focus.
- Effective Communication.
- Problem Solving.
- Personal Responsibility.
- Resilience.

An assessor will use a checklist to score you on this section. To be successful, you must attain a set minimum score. A number of marks are available for each of the four questions, and you must provide evidence for all of them. It is not, therefore, good enough to mark an answer with a comment similar to 'I have no experience in this area and so I am unable to answer the question'.

It is vital you write neatly in this section – if the assessor cannot read your answer, how can he or she score it? Also be careful with your spelling, grammar and punctuation. Practising on the photocopies will pay dividends in this section: you are not allowed to use continuation sheets and any writing outside the space provided will not be marked.

You can use examples from your private, work or educational life. This should give you ample opportunities to answer the questions. However, read the *entire* question before you answer, not just the broad title above it. Once you have read the question, think of a number of events/incidents/situations you feel would provide you with a suitable answer. Make notes on each and consider whether the event/incident/situation would provide you with adequate information to answer the question comprehensively.

In choosing what information to give in your answer always make sure of the following.

- That it doesn't just give theory.

- It gives a specific example.

- The example relates to you.

- It explains what you did, not what you might have done.

- The focus of your answer must always be on you and what you did – even if it is a team question explain what you did and how it affected the team and the outcome.

- Ensure that the example you use allows you to fully answer all parts of the question.

- That unless asked for, do not use more than the one example to answer the question fully.

When you have read the main question that asks you to recall a situation, consider the sub-questions. These ask for further details. Write these in the boxes provided. Remember, only complete the actual application form after a friend or relative has checked your draft answer for content, spelling, punctuation and grammar. The following is an example of how a situation can be used to provide evidence for this section of the form.

Michael is a 21-year-old student studying for a degree in geography. His course will end in the next three months. He is at the stage of his degree course that involves a number of field trips. Consequently, he has to work not only as part of a team but also on his own. He is a member of his local rugby club and regularly plays on a Saturday afternoon. To help fund his degree course, he has a part-time job in a local supermarket stacking shelves. He works shifts but he makes sure they do not interfere with his university work.

Michael can draw on events/incidents/situations that have occurred during his degree course, sporting activities and part-time job. Therefore, if a question on the application form was worded as follows he would be able to draw on all three activities:

It is vitally important that police officers work as part of a team. Please recall an example when you have worked as part of a team and your contribution ensured that the team met its goals or targets.

Describe the situation

I was working late one evening in the supermarket when a couple of people rang in to say they were too ill to attend work. This resulted in the team of shelf stackers being short staffed. We were expecting a large delivery that had to be unloaded quickly as the lorry had other stores to attend. The warehouse staff would unload the lorry but it was our responsibility to have the goods displayed on the relevant shelves before the store closed for the night.

What exactly did you do in the situation described?

I suggested to the other shelf stackers that we divide the store into areas. This would mean we would not waste time moving around the store – time that would be better spent stacking the shelves. We would then have a better chance to complete the job before the store closed. They agreed this was the best way to tackle the problem. I then suggested that we have a look to see exactly what had been delivered and then decide which areas of the store required our attention. Once we had examined the delivery and were aware of the aisles where the goods had to be stacked, I allocated each one of us an area of the store.

What was the result of your actions?

Although it was hard work we got the goods to the correct aisles and shelves in the time we had available to us. This meant the store was ready for opening the following day. The store manager thanked us all for our efforts. She particularly thanked me for organising the team. Since this occurred we now follow the same method with every delivery.

What do you think the consequences would have been if you had not acted in the way described?

The shelves would not have been stacked in time for the store closing. This would have resulted in someone having to do the work when he or she arrived the following morning. This would have had an effect on our team's reputation. The store may not have been ready for customers arriving, which would also have had an effect on the store's reputation. If customers could not buy the goods they wanted on this occasion they might consider doing their shopping elsewhere.

In this example the applicant has used an incident from his work experience to good effect in answering the questions posed. He has read the questions and answered each in a brief but informative manner.

TOP TIPS

- Double check your spelling and grammar.

- Photocopy the application form a number of times.

- Read the question and sub-questions carefully then formulate your answer.

- Practise writing your answer to ensure it fits into the space provided on the application form.

- Make sure your answer is legible. If the assessor cannot read it you will not be rewarded for your answer.

- Use examples from your personal, work or private life.

- Ensure that the examples used allow you to focus on you and what you did.

- Stick to one example per question unless it specifically asks for more.

- Have another person check your application form.

INDIVIDUAL LEARNING POINTS

_____

_____

_____

_____

_____

_____

_____

_____

_____

Chapter 4
Assessment Centres

Introduction

This chapter considers Assessment Centres and suggests some do's and don'ts about the centres that should ensure you avoid any pitfalls and understand what is expected of you.

It is not unusual to feel ill at ease in such situations as this, and you will not be the only person who is feeling nervous. However, take heart from the fact that the Assessment Centre has been designed to allow you to demonstrate your skills and abilities in full, not to catch you out. One of the strengths of an Assessment Centre is that it is a clear and transparent process: there are no tricks or hidden agendas.

Exercises and tests

During your time at the Assessment Centre, you will be expected to complete the following.

- Four interactive exercises.
- Two written exercises.
- An interview comprising of four questions.
- A verbal logical reasoning test.
- A numeracy test.

The order in which you will be asked to complete the exercises and tests will be given to you on the day. A set time is allowed for each exercise and test. The verbal logical reasoning and numeracy tests are often referred to as PIRT (Police Initial Recruit Tests).

Interactive and written exercises

When you are completing these, you will be asked to fulfil a job role in a named organisation. As an example and for the purposes of this book you will be a 'First Contact Officer' in a National Health Trust when completing tasks for the written and interactive exercises.

The job role you are given and the organisation are always fictitious. This is to ensure that all candidates are given the same opportunity. You will be provided with a full outline of the job role and its responsibilities. In addition, you will be given background information regarding the organisation and its policies that may be of benefit to you.

Once you are familiar with the role and the exercises, you will see that they are very similar to the role of a police officer and to the situations and tasks that police officers are required to deal with.

Throughout the assessment process, no legal knowledge or police experience is required or expected.

Interviews

For the interview you are expected to be yourself. When questioned regarding your previous experiences, you can use examples from your work, education or leisure activities. As the assessors have no prior knowledge of the candidates, if appropriate, you can use the answers you gave to the questions during the written application stage.

Verbal logical reasoning and numeracy tests

There are two tests. One tests your basic mathematics and the other your ability to read, understand and reach appropriate conclusions from information provided. Both these tests take the form of multiple-choice question papers. (Full explanations and examples of all these exercises and tests are provided in the relevant chapters of this book.)

What you will receive before you attend

You will be notified in writing of the date, time and location of your Assessment Centre. In addition, you will be sent two documents.

- A brief explanation of the Assessment Centre.

- The background information and job role you are required to fulfil when completing the written and interactive exercises.

You will be sent these documents at least two weeks before you attend for assessment. You will be asked before the assessment begins if you have received these documents. If not, you will be asked if you want to continue with the assessment or whether you want to be rescheduled until you have had the time to receive and digest the information.

Remember that some forces may only hold Assessment Centres one week in every six months, depending on their recruiting requirements. If this is the case for the force you have applied to, it could delay your application for a considerable time. If you have not received the full information but decide to go ahead anyway, should you not be successful, you will not be allowed to appeal on these grounds. If you have been preparing in advance of your receiving this material (e.g. by getting the documents from the web or other sources), it is important that you check to see whether any alterations have been made when the material arrives.

Check the time, date and location of the Assessment Centre. The assessment will start at the stated time and, if you arrive once it has commenced, you may be unable to take part. If this happens you will have to wait for a future appointment. As mentioned above, if you miss your allotted slot you may have to wait a lengthy period of time for another appointment.

The information you are sent will list the documents you should take with you as evidence of your identity. Make sure you take these with you – failure to do so may prevent you from taking part. These documents include a full 10-year passport or two of the following.

- A British driving licence.

- A P45.

- A birth certificate issued within six weeks of your birth.

- A cheque book and bank card with three statements and proof of signature.

- A credit card containing a photograph of yourself.

- Proof of residence (e.g. a council tax or utility bill).

Illness

Whether the Assessment Centre is operated by an individual police service or a group of services, it represents a large investment in terms of money and resources. Should you become ill prior to attending for an assessment, it is very important that you contact the service to which you have applied as soon as possible. This will give the service the opportunity to fill the space created by your non-attendance.

Before the assessment begins, you will be asked if you are fit and well. If you feel ill, this is the time to say, so that your Assessment Centre can be rescheduled. If you commence the assessment but have to withdraw, this will normally be classed as your being unsuccessful.

Candidates with specific needs

If you have a physical disability, you should talk directly to the police service to which you have applied regarding what is, or is not, considered to be a bar to service. If you have a temporary disability, you should still speak to the service to which you have applied about the nature of your disability and the restrictions this may cause in terms of preventing you from performing to the best of your abilities during the assessment. Every effort will be made to change either the physical location or the structure of the Assessment Centre to ensure fairness to all candidates.

Should you have a specific learning disability, such as dyslexia, this will be taken into account during the assessment. For this to happen, however, you should inform the relevant police service. They will ask you to submit a report outlining your learning difficulty. This report should be completed by a specialist in adult learning difficulties.

This report is studied by a psychologist who will make recommendations, if appropriate, for changes to the structure of the Assessment Centre. An example of such an adjustment for a candidate with dyslexia would be for him or her to be awarded an extra 25 per cent time for the written exercises and for the preparation parts (reading) of the interactive exercises.

If you reveal after the assessment that you have a specific learning need, this will not be taken into account in the marking. It will also not be allowed as grounds for appeal in the event of your being unsuccessful.

Travelling to the Assessment Centre

As mentioned above, if you are late arriving you may be prevented from taking part. So make sure you plan your journey in advance, leaving yourself plenty of time for any unforeseen hold-ups. The best way to do this is to undertake a practice journey, preferably at a similar time to when you will travel on the assessment day. Remember, if you do a practice run at the weekend, it may take you much longer on a weekday.

Whether travelling by car or public transport, always ensure you have enough time so that you arrive in a calm manner. If you are unsure whether the Assessment Centre has parking, then check this prior to attending. Having to find alternative parking could add a considerable amount to your total journey time.

Arriving at the Assessment Centre

When you arrive, you will usually be placed in a group of eight candidates. You will stay with this group when you do the interactive exercises and interviews. Depending on the size of the room, you may join other groups to complete the remaining tests and written exercises.

Although you will be assigned to a group, you will be required to complete all the exercises and tests on your own.

What to wear

You should be comfortable throughout the assessment, so consider carefully what you intend to wear – you do not want to be too hot or too cold. While you are not judged on your appearance, you have to complete the exercises carrying out a specified job role. Some candidates feel comfortable when completing these exercises wearing clothing appropriate to the role they are required to fulfil. Most candidates, therefore, wear smart clothes.

Avoid carrying bags as these can be a distraction. Likewise, you will be asked to turn off your mobile phone and you will not be allowed to take it with you to any part of the Assessment Centre. So, if possible, leave your mobile phone at home.

GENERAL ASSUMPTION

During the assessment you will be assessed on your appearance.

FACT

Although your clothes should be clean, you are not judged on your appearance unless it is totally inappropriate. This would include, for example, wearing a T-shirt with obscene words on it.

Dress to feel at your best but comfortable. Should you wear, for example, a tie and jacket and then, on the day of your assessment, it becomes very warm, do not be afraid to remove these. It will not affect your assessment in any way.

How to behave

Always treat other candidates and Assessment Centre staff in an appropriate manner, from the moment you arrive to the moment you leave. The ability to treat all people with dignity and respect is a skill all police officers must be able to display. (We will look at this in greater detail in **Chapter 8**.)

GENERAL ASSUMPTION

Your behaviour is only assessed during exercises or tests.

FACT

While this is true, inappropriate behaviour will be taken into consideration at any time you are at the Assessment Centre, even if you have been told you are on a break. Such behaviour may be taken into account when considering your suitability for an appointment. This may seem unfair, but it is based on the fact that, once appointed as a constable, you are never off duty – you have to be aware of your behaviour and actions at all times. It would therefore be wrong for a police service to observe unacceptable behaviour and not take this into consideration when making an appointment.

It is difficult to give a list of appropriate and inappropriate behaviour. What you should do is consider the location, audience and circumstances in which any behaviour is being displayed. Police officers must be able to adapt to many situations and react appropriately to them all.

As an example, consider swearing. Can you think of a time and place when it would be acceptable for a police officer to swear? Even if you can think of an occasion when swearing may be justified, this does not mean that swearing is acceptable at any time. As a general rule, if in doubt, don't do it!

Briefings during the assessment

All candidates will receive information in the form of verbal briefings at the start of the assessment and then at the beginning of each exercise and test. When giving briefings, the centre's staff read from prepared cards. This may seem strange, but it does ensure you receive the same information as all the other candidates.

At key points in a briefing, you will be given written cards to read to reinforce what you are being told. This will help you understand the key points.

At the end of a briefing, if you are unsure, ask. It is almost certain that others in your group will also be unclear. Asking questions during briefings will not affect your assessment in any way. The invigilators who give the briefings are not involved in the assessment, but they will report on any inappropriate behaviour they observe. The invigilators will do their best to ensure you feel at ease and will make sure you are in the right place for each part of the assessment.

Approaching the exercises and tests

You should attend the Assessment Centre with an open mind, confident that you have the required skills – after all, you will have demonstrated some of these skills in getting through the paper application. Use the skills you have, not a set method for completing the written and interactive exercises. The only formula – such as it is – is to respond appropriately to what you read and to what you are told.

In the interactive exercises, do not assume that the racial origin or sex of the role player is part of the exercise: most exercises are not race or gender specific. Should race or sex be part of the exercise, this will be made clear in the exercise materials.

> **GENERAL ASSUMPTION**
>
> You should adopt a definite system for the assessment exercises. Using a set system or method, or getting in certain buzz words or phrases, is the recipe for success.

> **FACT**
>
> Police work is complicated, if only for the fact that people are involved and no two people are alike. People have different expectations and needs. Equally, no two police officers are the same, and so there is often no right or wrong answer, or just one way of dealing with a policing situation. The same is true of the exercises at the Assessment Centre. Any system will have its weaknesses, and preconceived words or phrases will not help if they are not applicable to the situation or person.
>
> Having said this, what you can do is develop skills and abilities so that you can respond appropriately to what you read or hear. We will explore this further when we consider the interactive and written exercises in detail.

Refreshments

Most assessments take about five hours. However, the facilities at each Assessment Centre vary – some offer refreshments but others are unable to do so, although all should provide drinking water. The Assessment Centre will tell you in advance if you are allowed to bring food with you.

You will know from personal experience that too much food can make you feel tired and lethargic. So avoid overeating. Similarly, even if you feel nervous it is usually better to eat something rather than go for a long period without food. This is particularly important if you made an early start and so did without breakfast.

Comfort breaks

Comfort breaks will be offered throughout the assessment. It is important you take advantage of these because, if you need to take a break at any time during an exercise or test, you will not be allowed any extra time to complete these on your return.

Speaking to other candidates

There are no tasks that require you to consult with the other candidates. So formal exam conditions apply to all the tests and exercises. Between exercises, however, you are allowed to speak to the other candidates, but avoid being drawn into conversations regarding what has taken place or what happens next. The Assessment Centre is about your completing the exercises, tests and interview to the best of your own abilities.

Listening to what others have done will, at best, confirm that what you did was the same as others or, at worst, cause you to have doubts. If you discuss future exercises, this may cause you to be indecisive or to do something you may not otherwise have done. It is very unlikely this would be to your advantage. Therefore, restrict any conversations you have with the other candidates to small talk. Should you hear discussions about the exercises and tests, try to avoid listening and certainly do not join in.

It is worth repeating that, as well as avoiding entering into conversations at the Assessment Centre, you should be very careful about obtaining information from websites or others who have previously completed the assessment, even if they have been successful.

If you have preconceived ideas about the exercises, it is likely you will have made up your mind as to the actions and decisions you will take. This may stop you asking appropriate questions or listening to what you are being told, and this will consequently impact negatively on your performance.

TOP TIPS

- Make sure you take with you the required identification evidence.

- Make sure you have received and have read the latest information documents.

- Discuss any specific needs you may have prior to attending for your assessment.

- Know the route (and any alternative routes) to the Assessment Centre.

- Allow plenty of time for travelling.

- Dress appropriately but make sure you are comfortable.

- At all times treat everyone with dignity and respect.

- Have sufficient refreshment prior to assessment.

- Take advantage of comfort breaks.

- Avoid discussions with your fellow candidates.

- Be wary of information you are given by candidates who have attended previously.

- Be wary of information contained in unofficial websites.

INDIVIDUAL LEARNING POINTS

_____

_____

_____

_____

_____

_____

_____

_____

_____

_____

Chapter 5
Interactive Exercises

Introduction

The interactive exercises involve you role playing someone who has a specific job in an organisation. You will be provided with information concerning a situation or an incident that has occurred in this organisation, and you will have to deal with someone who is involved in this situation or incident in some way, role playing the person whose job you have been given.

Each interactive exercise is made up of two five-minute parts. There is a 90-second gap between each part. In the first part, you prepare for the role play on your own. In the second, you meet the person who is role acting the other part in the situation or incident, and it is in this part that you must deal with his or her issue or concern. There are four interactive exercises in total, each lasting $11\frac{1}{2}$ minutes. The number of exercises may be increased or reduced, but the principles behind them will remain the same.

Your role

Before you attend the Assessment Centre you will be sent an outline of the job you will role play, along with any background information you may require. This will also include the details of any policies relevant to the organisation on which the exercises are based. You should read and try to understand these, but you do not need to learn them off by heart. If you want to refer to these during the exercises, they will be available for you to consult. It is, however, important that you have a good grasp of these before you attend.

In addition to receiving the job description and the background material, you will also receive a brief explanation of the Assessment Centre. This will contain the names of the four interactive exercises you will be required to undertake. After the name of each exercise will be a brief description of that exercise (for example, 'Allen wishes to discuss an incident he witnessed at the hospital').

Part one of an interactive exercise

In this part of the exercise you are given written information about the issue or incident and about the person you will meet (an example of this material is provided later in this chapter). Always read this information slowly and deliberately so that you are clear as to what it is you are being asked to do.

You will be provided with paper and pens so that you can make notes. While you are not allowed to take the original information with you to part two of the exercise, you can take your notes. These are not assessed.

Use your notes to:

- write down any key points;

- write down any points that require clarification;

- identify any appropriate questions;

- identify any information that should be given by you to the role actor; and

- identify potential options for dealing with the situation.

Simply list these points briefly so that you can use them as reminders. Do not make too many notes. If you do, you will not be able to pick out the key points when you meet the role actor. Try to keep your notes to no more than one side of A4. Keep them clear, simple and easy to read.

Part two of an interactive exercise

You will enter a room where you will meet the person you are required to deal with. Also in this room, seated, will be an assessor. If a third person is present, he or she is there to monitor the exercise, not you. This person will also be seated, close to the assessor. The person you will speak to will be very evident as he or she will be wearing a name badge appropriate to the exercise. This person will usually speak to you when you enter the room.

On a chair near to the role actor will be a copy of the information you read in part one. It will be the same: you do not need to check to see if it contains changed or additional information. Should you need to refer to this information, do so.

When dealing with the role actor, do not be afraid to use your notes to make sure you raise all the issues and questions you need to raise. Do not be afraid to take the time to do this: you are not required to fill silences, however tempting this may be, and you are not penalised for periods of silence. If appropriate, use the chair provided to sit on. One will also have been provided for the role actor. It is usually appropriate to remain seated throughout the five minutes.

You are not allowed to write during part two of the exercise. Should you do so, you will be reminded at the end of the five minutes not to do so. No further action will be taken.

GENERAL ASSUMPTION

The exercises are unfair because you would not normally deal with such issues within a five-minute period.

FACT

You are only required to do what is possible within the five minutes. You can score very well even if you do not reach a conclusion.

The checklists the assessors use to monitor your performance were devised after watching numerous mock candidates complete the exercises within the same time frame. Like you, these mock candidates will have been provided with only five minutes' preparation time and five minutes' activity time.

These mock candidates are selected from newly appointed police officers in their first few weeks of training, so they should reflect the potential actions and behaviours of would-be candidates. What the majority of these mock candidates were able to achieve within the five minutes is reflected in the assessors' marking guides.

Moving from one exercise to the next

You will be fully briefed before beginning the interactive exercises. All candidates are required to complete four exercises in total. This represents eight periods of five minutes, with 90 seconds between each. Candidates complete the exercises in syndicates of eight, although every individual candidate completes each exercise alone.

A buzzer or whistle signals the end of each five minutes or 90 seconds. Do not worry if you do not hear the signal: an assessor will ensure you move at the appropriate time and to the right place. Each of the four exercises is standalone. You do not, therefore, need to take any information from one exercise to the next.

During the briefing you will be given an exercise starting number (this is part of the candidate number that was allocated to you at the start of the Assessment Centre). The preparation areas are numbered 1, 3, 5 and 7. Preparation areas are either a room (next to the appropriate activity room) or a desk in a corridor outside the room in which you will undertake the activity. Activity rooms are numbered 2, 4, 6 and 8.

Following the briefing, candidates who have odd numbers commence the activities by going to the preparation area indicated by their numbers. They will then move through the exercises numerically until they have completed all of them. For example, an odd-numbered candidate starts at preparation area number 3. He or she will then move to activity room number 4 and will then proceed through all subsequent preparation and activity rooms to finish at number 2.

Candidates who have even numbers are taken on to the assessment floor five minutes after the odd-numbered candidates. They are told to begin at the number one up from their candidate number. For example, a candidate has been allocated the number 2. When he or she is taken on to the assessment floor, he or she will begin at number 3. Number 8, however, will start at number 1. The reason for this is that candidates can only commence at a preparation part of an exercise.

The interactive exercise assessment floor will be laid out similar to the diagram below. You move round the exercises as indicated by the arrows.

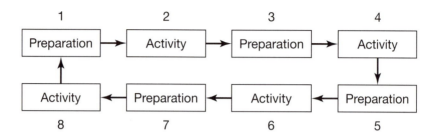

Example exercise

Before continuing, read the information pack in **Appendix C**. You should understand the role you are required to fulfil and the policies relevant to your role and the organisation.

Now read the sample exercise called 'Cox'. Try to keep this reading to five minutes to reflect Assessment Centre conditions. Make any notes you think appropriate in the space labelled 'Candidate notes'. Keep these short. Remember, if this was an exercise at an Assessment Centre, the printed information would be available to you in both parts of the exercise, so you do not have to record too much detail. Make notes to jog your memory about those things you would want to say or ask the role actor, and about your potential solutions.

Interactive exercise

Cox

Candidate information

In this exercise there are three pages of information.

1   A general report from Hilary Dornan, the First Contact Manager.
2   A visitor's information report.
3   A copy of the Central Trust's Equality Policy Statement.

Following the preparation period, you will meet Ashley Cox.

Central Hospital Trust

General report

From: Hilary Dornan, First Contact Manager
To: Candidate, First Contact Officer
Date: Yesterday
Subject: Ashley Cox

A report was made to the Ward Sister by Susan Haddock yesterday when she visited an elderly relative. This report was passed on to me for action. A copy is attached for your information.

Ashley Cox has worked here for approximately nine months, and inquiries suggest he was working in the relevant area yesterday afternoon.

I have arranged for you to meet with Ashley Cox to discuss what took place.

To assist you, I have attached a copy of the Trust's Equality Policy.

Hilary Dornan

Hilary Dornan

First Contact Manager

Central Hospital Trust

Visitors' information report

Person reporting issue/incident: Susan Haddock
Address: 1 Provenance Road
Central Town
CT1 1AN

Date information received: Yesterday at 2.00 pm

On walking through the hospital near to the Dryden Ward to visit an elderly relative, Susan Haddock saw two painters, one shouting inappropriate things to the other. She was particularly concerned because she had her six-year-old son with her and she did not want him to hear such things.

She heard one of the painters say: 'Coxy, don't be such a thick paddy.' Apparently they had painted over some masking tape. The same man then made some comment about 'his lot' all being members of the IRA. The other painter made no effort to stop the other speaking to him like this.

Susan Haddock cannot understand why, in a hospital of all places, members of staff speak to each other in this way and was concerned that, if children hear such things, they will think that it is right to make such jokes or comments. She felt most strongly that she should report such behaviour and that hospital management should take appropriate action.

J Suffolk

J Suffolk
Ward Sister

Central Hospital Trust

Equality Policy Statement

It is intended that all staff, patients and visitors should follow this Policy. This Policy requires that no one on the hospital premises should receive less favourable treatment or be discriminated against because of:

- Gender
- Marital status
- Religion
- Political opinion
- Race
- Sexual orientation
- Disability
- Age
- Gender reassignment
- Nationality.

All Trust employees should note and challenge behaviour that is in breach of this Policy. Should they not be able to do so or should it be considered inappropriate to challenge the behaviour at that time, it should be reported to their Line Manager.

This relates to both employment opportunities and the health services provided by the Trust.

Discrimination includes harassment, which means unwelcome or unwanted behaviour.

Any such behaviour is totally unacceptable.

Anyone who feels they are being treated unfairly or without respect should take action. The following are suggestions, although this is not an exhaustive list:

1 Tell the person to stop (they may not know they are behaving inappropriately).

2 Talk to someone else, a manager or friend. They may be able to offer advice or assistance in seeking a resolution. A First Contact Officer will always be a point of contact and will be independent.

3 Make a formal complaint. This should be made in writing to the First Contact Manager.

The Policy seeks to ensure that legislation and the Trust's Policy are complied with and to ensure that everyone is treated with respect and dignity.

Candidate's notes

Having completed your preparation for this exercise, look at your notes and the questions you have prepared. Have you considered asking Ashley Cox the following?

- Where was he working yesterday?

- Was he working with anyone else?

- Did anything untoward happen?

- Exactly what was said?

- Were members of the public present?

- How does he get on with the person he was working with?

- The other person's name?

- Has he worked with that person before?

- Have there been other incidents with that person or with other members of staff?

Also consider those things you would want to tell the role actor, such as the following.

- The other employee's behaviour was totally unacceptable.

- The key points from the Trust's Equality Statement.

- The fact that it is unacceptable for anyone, particularly a visitor with a child, to witness this type of behaviour.

- That everyone in the Trust has a duty to help stop such behaviour.

Lastly, have you considered potential solutions?

- What does Cox want to happen?

- Does he know the options available to him?

- How does he wish to proceed, considering the options?

- What are the potential options for feeding back to the person who reported it?

This may appear a lot to consider in five minutes, but most candidates readily process the key questions and issues within this time limit. Remember, make a list only: you usually do not have the time to write out your notes in full. As an alternative to writing your questions separately, you could list general areas, such as the following.

- Who was there?

- What happened?

- Their relationships with the co-worker and other employees.

- Whether there have been other incidents.

Similarly, you could record key words for the issues you wish to raise and for your suggested solutions.

The 90-second interval

During this time you will move from the preparation area to go to stand outside the activity room where you will meet the role actor. This will literally take seconds. Use the remaining time to consider a structure for dealing with the role actor, but remember that you are not allowed to write during the 90 seconds.

A structured format for dealing with this and similar exercises would be as follows.

- *Collect information from the role actor*: first, ask the role actor appropriate questions to obtain all the information you require to understand fully what happened and to establish who else was present.

- *Give the role actor information*: give the role actor any information he or she appears not to have and outline any appropriate policies or issues.

- *Discuss potential solutions*: in consultation with the role actor, explore potential solutions to the situation. If appropriate, consider short, medium and long-term solutions.

- *State your proposed actions*: outline your intended course of action. In addition, identify whom you intend to give feedback to and how this will take place. Where possible, gain agreement from the role actor with regards to your proposed course of action. Do not be put off if the role actor does not give his or her definite approval – it would be unusual for him or her to do so.

What happens during the second part of the exercise?

After 90 seconds, on hearing the signal, enter the room and deal with the role actor as you think appropriate. You do not need to knock before entering, and you will see the role actor you are required to deal with. (As mentioned previously, he or she will have a badge that clearly identifies him or her.)

The role actor will usually have an opening line to deliver to you. After he or she has delivered this, talk to him or her as you would to anyone else during a normal conversation. Try to control any nerves you may have and listen to what the role actor is saying. Resist the temptation to start talking immediately as this will stop the role actor from delivering his or her first line. Do not be afraid to use your notes or the provided printed exercise information.

Should you dry up during the five minutes, the role actor will look away to the floor. If this happens, the assessor will tell you that you can start talking again if you wish at any time during the five minutes. You are not penalised for pauses, however long. When you start again, no explanation or apology is required: just continue as if there had been no break. The role actor will immediately re-engage with you.

The signal will then be given that indicates the end of the exercise. If you continue after this signal, the assessor will simply ask you to leave the room. Do not, therefore, try to continue, as nothing you say after the five minutes will be scored and you are reducing the time you have available to move to the next preparation area or room.

How behaviours are scored

The assessor looks at his or her checklist to see if the questions or statements you make or ask are listed there. If they are, the relevant question or statement is ticked as having been achieved. On the assessor's checklist your questions and statements are referred to as 'behaviours'.

There are usually between 12 and 18 behaviours on an exercise checklist. Groups of similar behaviours are listed together under the appropriate competency area. If you look at the suggested questions and statements for the sample exercise 'Cox', the first set would be recorded under the heading 'Problem Solving', the second under 'Effective Communication' and the third under 'Community and Customer Focus'.

If you look at the National Core Competencies listed in **Appendix A**, you will see how the groups of behaviours relate to those areas. As an example, consider the first set of questions. If you look at the positive indicators under the competency area 'Problem Solving', you will see how asking those questions would relate to the following positive indicators.

- Gets as much information as is appropriate on all aspects of a problem.

- Separates relevant information from irrelevant information, and important information from unimportant information.

- Takes in information quickly and accurately.

- Reviews all the information gathered to understand the situation and draws logical conclusions.

In addition to scoring the behaviours, the assessors have to decide how well each individual behaviour was achieved. The assessors are given clear guidelines about this during their training, and they are also given descriptors (called 'scalars') within the bounds of which their decisions must be taken.

Consider again the questions from the Cox example. The scalar used for these questions would be something like 'thorough to vague'. For example, you have spoken with the role actor and have established that he was indeed painting near to Dryden Ward at 2.00 pm when some inappropriate things were said. You now want to find out exactly what was said. You could achieve this by asking one of the following questions.

- 'With regards to the inappropriate comments, can you please tell me exactly what was said?'

- 'Can you please give me a brief outline of what was said?'

- 'Did he say something about the IRA?'

- 'Was something said to you?'

All these examples are ways of finding out what was said, but the first is thorough, the second less so and the final two are vague. As a general rule, if you say exactly what is on the checklist, you will be awarded a mid-point scalar score.

GENERAL ASSUMPTION

You do better if you score lots of behaviours on the assessor's checklist.

FACT

What you do (behaviours) and how you do them (scalars) are of equal importance. Therefore, you can perform a few of the identified behaviours well, yet still score the same (or better) than someone who does lots of behaviours badly. The reason for this is simple: in dealing with the public it is very often not what you do that is important, but how you actually do it. Many complaints against the police are not based on what officers actually did but the way they did them.

The area Respect for Race and Diversity and a candidate's oral communication skills are also assessed in the interactive exercises, but usually without descriptive behaviours.

How Respect for Race and Diversity is scored

Respect for Race and Diversity is taken into consideration for everything you do during the five minutes you interact with the role actor. There are, however, usually no stated behaviours for the assessor to monitor. All your statements and questions can be considered, and the assessors will have been provided with instructions to guide their observations. This normally takes the form of two short, descriptive sentences. Using the example 'Cox', these would typically be as follows.

- Deals with the role actor in a sensitive way.

- Uses appropriate language and terms with regards to all the involved parties and issues.

In addition to these sentences, scalars are also used. Again using 'Cox' as an example:

- Sentence 1 would be 'Sensitive' to 'Insensitive'.

- Sentence 2 would be 'Appropriate' to 'Inappropriate'.

If your actions do not fall within the prescribed parameters for assessment, but the behaviour you display is inappropriate, this will still be recorded and could result in your being awarded a grade D (this is explained in more detail in **Chapter 8**).

How your oral communication skills are scored

The assessors are asked to consider two things about the way you speak.

- Can they hear what you say?

- Can they understand what you are saying?

49

The assessors will do this by taking into account factors similar to those listed below.

- Can the candidate be heard?

- Can the candidate be understood?

- Is the language used inappropriate or jargon?

- Is there structure to it?

- Is it appropriate for the audience?

- Are the responses appropriate to the other person?

- Does the candidate interrupt and over-talk?

As in the competency area Respect for Race and Diversity, this is described in two sentences.

- Can be heard and is structured and logical.

- Uses appropriate language.

Again, there would be two scalars.

- Sentence 1 would be 'Clear' to 'Unclear'.

- Sentence 2 would be 'Appropriate' to 'Inappropriate'.

These factors will be taken into consideration for everything you say during the five minutes. You should not worry too much about structure, even if you are following a definite plan – just make sure you respond appropriately to the role actor. You will not be penalised in any way for deviating from your plan.

This part of the assessment is simply to ensure that you can be understood and that you can link questions and answers logically together. Most candidates have no difficulty in achieving the required standard in this area.

Example assessor's checklist

Below is an example of an assessor's checklist using the 'Cox' exercise. On the left are the behaviours the assessors are looking for you to demonstrate. In the middle are the scalar descriptors for scoring a behaviour. On the right are the grade options (A–D).

'Cox' exercise checklist

Behaviours	Scalars	Grade
Problem Solving		A, B, C, D
1.1 Asks where he or she worked yesterday	Thorough to Vague	
1.2 Asks whom he or she was with	Thorough to Vague	
1.3 Asks what was said	Thorough to Vague	
1.4 Asks whether members of the public were present	Thorough to Vague	

Behaviours	Scalars	Grade
1.5 Asks whether this type of behaviour has happened previously	Thorough to Vague	
1.6 Asks whether this behaviour is limited to just this individual or to others	Thorough to Vague	
Community and Customer Focus		A, B, C, D
2.1 States such behaviour is unacceptable	Clear to Unclear	
2.2 Outlines the Equality Policy	Clear to Unclear	
2.3 Asks role actor how he or she would like this resolved	Clear to Unclear	
Effective Communication		A, B, C, D
3.1 States he or she will deal with this in partnership with the role actor	Confident to Unsure	
3.2 Clearly outlines the options for resolution	Confident to Unsure	
3.3 Identifies that such language and behaviour breach the Equality Policy	Confident to Unsure	
Respect for Race and Diversity		A, B, C, D
4.1 Deals with the role actor in a sensitive way	Sensitive to Insensitive	
4.2 Uses appropriate language and terms in dealing with the individual and issues	Appropriate to Inappropriate	
Oral communication skills		A, B, C, D
5.1 Can be heard and is structured and logical	Clear to Unclear	
5.2 Uses appropriate language	Appropriate to Inappropriate	

How a competency area is scored

At the end of the five minutes the assessor considers each competency area in turn, noting how many behaviours the candidate has scored and how well these were performed. Scalars are assessed on a scale of 1–5 (1 being the highest score). From these two scores, the candidate is awarded a grade for that competency area, from A to D (A being the highest).

An example for Problem Solving is as follows. A candidate demonstrates only one behaviour by saying 'Was something said to you?'. This behaviour would be marked as scored at 1.3 on the checklist. The assessor would then decide how thoroughly or vaguely the question was asked. It would be scored 1 if it was considered totally thorough and 5 if vague. In this case, it would probably be given a score of 5: the candidate did not ask *what* was said but whether something had been said. As a general rule, it is always best to ask open questions – questions that, usually, cannot be answered with just one word.

Think of how a parent might ask his or her child about the child's day at school. The parent could ask: 'Did you have a good day at school?' This is a closed question – he or she would probably receive a one-word answer (yes or no). If the parent asked an open question ('What did you do at school today?'), this should receive a more detailed answer.

The assessor looks at these two indicators (the behaviours and the scalar) and then awards a grade – in this case a D. This is because the candidate showed only one of the required behaviours in that competency area, and he or she did not do this very well.

A further example can be given using Community and Customer Focus. The candidate scores 2.1 by saying 'Gerard White's behaviour, as described, is unacceptable'. This would attract a scalar of 3 because the candidate did exactly what was on the checklist – no better or worse than the mid-point on the scalar. The candidate could then go on to score 2.2 by reading the Equality Policy Statement to the role actor. Because the candidate can do no more in terms of displaying this behaviour, he or she would most likely attract a scalar of 1. These two scores produce an average scalar for that competency area of 2. The final grade is calculated by combining the overall scalar with the number of behaviours scored. In this example it would score a B.

With regards to Respect for Race and Diversity and oral communication skills, the assessor will consider what the candidate said during the five minutes. He or she will use the sentence descriptors and the scalars to award a grade for each of these.

As can be seen from these examples, you do not have to say exactly what is on the checklist in order to score. In addition, you can ask questions or make statements at any time during the five minutes, and this will not affect the grade you will achieve. For example, early in the five minutes a candidate scores a 1.1 and a 1.4. Towards the end of the five minutes, the candidate asks the question relating to behaviour 1.6. The fact that the candidate did not ask the questions as a group will not affect how the assessor considers the scalars for each question and the candidate's overall grade.

The role actors

In addition to training in assessment and role acting, the role actors are trained in the exercises they will perform. They aim to give the same performance for each candidate: they will not react in any way to the candidate's actions and attitudes, other than to give the prescribed responses to the statements made or the questions asked. They respond in the manner they have been asked to portray.

The role actors are given background information regarding the roles they will play, plus set responses to the candidates' questions and statements. These set responses are derived from observing mock candidates during the design and development of that particular exercise. A role actor will usually have between 12 and 20 lines. They must learn these off by heart so that each candidate receives the same information. In addition, the role actors must understand the potential questions and statements from candidates so that they can deliver the prescribed lines at the correct time.

Below is an example of a role actor's instructions for the 'Cox' exercise. Obviously you will not see these instructions, but they will show you what type of information the role actor receives and should give you the confidence that all candidates receive the same experiences and opportunities.

Role actor's instructions

Background information

Your name is Ashley Cox and you have worked as a decorator for the Central Hospital Trust for nine months. You were born in Belfast in Northern Ireland but left 20 years ago when you came to live in England. Since then you have worked for various organisations but always as a painter and decorator.

You live in Central Town with your partner and two children, a boy and a girl aged 10 and 8 years, respectively.

For health and safety reasons, decorators are required to work in pairs and, since commencing at the hospital, you have always worked with Gerard White, who, you believe, has worked for the Trust for nine years.

White has always made comments regarding your origin of birth. As you did not initially challenge this, you now feel unable to say anything. You do not find it humorous, but actually quite insulting.

You have no religious or political allegiances and have always adopted a stance of not getting into such conversations. While you are generally unassertive, you are resolute regarding not getting drawn into such conversations, other than to say all groups must look forward to a peaceful future, and not back.

Yesterday you were painting near Dryden Ward at 2.00 pm with Gerard White. He made comments to you regarding 'thick paddies' and the IRA. You would not have raised this issue personally but now you would like it resolved, and you will be guided by the First Contact Officer regarding possible solutions. No other employees have made such comments.

Prompts and scripted lines

- When the candidates enter the room, say: 'My name is Ashley Cox. I understand that you want to see me.'

- If the candidate asks what happened, say: 'Just some comments were made.'

- If the candidate asks what was said, say: 'Something about being a thick paddy and the IRA.'

- If the candidate asks if anything else was said, say: 'It is just that sort of thing and Irish jokes.'

- If the candidate asks how many visitors or patients witnessed this or any such behaviour, say: 'I am not sure – it could be lots.'

- If the candidate asks what others would think of such behaviour, say: 'I don't really know, but it is not really professional.'

- If the candidate asks if other staff have witnessed such behaviour, say: 'Lots, but I couldn't say who heard it so I cannot give you any names.'

- If the candidate asks how it makes you feel, say: 'Well, it doesn't make me happy. In fact, it is quite uncomfortable.'

- If the candidate asks why you have not tried to stop it, say: 'I didn't say anything at first so it just became the norm. I don't feel I can tell Gerard to stop and I just think that he thinks he is being funny.'

- If the candidate explains the Equality Policy Statement, say: 'But it doesn't seem to make any difference to me.'

- If the candidate says such behaviour is unacceptable, say: 'But how can we make it stop?'

- If the candidate asks what you would like to be done, say: 'I'm not really sure. I'll be guided by you.'

- If the candidate asks why you think Gerard makes such comments, say: 'I think he is just ignorant. I don't think he means anything by it.'

You do not have to give the questions or statements as per the role actor's prompts in order to get the response, but they do have to have the same meaning. Should you ask questions or make statements that do not have a scripted line, the role actors will keep their answers as short as possible. However, their responses will be within the confines of the background information.

It is very important that you listen to what the role actor is saying and respond to this. While you will have a plan for dealing with the situation and will have considered what questions and statements you want to ask or make, you have to be flexible and must respond appropriately to the role actor.

What happens if you finish before the end of the five minutes?

You should not be concerned if you finish before the signal for the end of the exercise. As mentioned previously, should this happen, the role actor will simply look at the floor. You are not allowed to leave the room and, should you wish to start again at any time, simply recommence the conversation. You are not penalised for silences and nor should you try to engage the role actor or assessor in small talk as neither will respond. Even if you indicate that you have finished, the assessor will tell you that you can carry on at any time within the five minutes, should you wish to do so.

As a general rule, if you finish before the end, go back to the start and recap on what you and the role actor have said and agreed. This will assist your memory and can very often spur you on to ask further questions or to seek clarification (remember, you cannot score during a silence). Remember, many candidates finish before the end of the five minutes but still score very well.

What not to have with you

Bleepers and mobile phones

During the briefing for the interactive exercises, you will be told not to carry any items that give off sounds. This is to prevent candidates mistaking the sound these make for the sound that indicates the start or finish of the exercises. Some candidates think they can use bleepers or mobile phones as an alarm to signal they are nearing the end of the five minutes. This is not, however, allowed, and such devices will be taken from you if you try to use them in this way. While you will not be penalised for this, it may affect your concentration if you are told to turn off your bleeper or mobile phone.

Written information

In addition to bleepers and mobile phones, you are not allowed to take the information you were sent prior to attending the Assessment Centre or any notes you made before attending into the exercises and tests. Such information could give you an unfair advantage over the other candidates and, should you consult this information during your assessment, it is likely this would cause you to fail, no matter how well you perform in the assessment itself.

Further example interactive scenarios

Below are the outlines of two further example interactive exercises. Using a similar format to the one you used for the Cox exercise consider the issues and how you would want to deal with each situation. (Obviously to a certain extent that would be governed by the answers the role actor gives to your questions during the five minutes). Having done that consider your potential responses against the competencies.

Obviously you would not normally get in the written information the opening line the role actor would give as you enter the interactive room, however these have been included in the information so that you can understand the types of opening lines that you may hear.

Example Exercise 1

Interactive exercise

Farrow

Candidate information

In this exercise there are two pages of information.

1   A general report from Hilary Dornan, the First Contact Manager.

2   A visitor's information report.

General report

From: Hilary Dornan, First Contact Manager
To: Candidate, First Contact Officer
Date: Two days ago
Subject: Jane Farrow

Jane Farrow visited the hospital to see her ill father. She had her son with her. During the visit her son became lost and she has concerns about how the hospital assisted her to find her son and I have attached the report she made.

I have arranged for you to meet with Jane Farrow to discuss what took place.

Hilary Dornan

Hilary Dornan

First Contact Manager

Central Hospital Trust

Visitors' information report

Person reporting issue/incident: Jane Farrow

Address: 42 Bants Lane
Central Town
CT3 1AF

Date information received: Two days ago at 7 p.m.

This afternoon I visited my sick father who was being treated in your hospital. Because of personal circumstances I had to bring my son, Ben, with me who is only five years old. After about fifteen minutes my Dad asked for a drink and he can no longer do this without assistance so rather than call for a nurse I attempted to help him but while doing this lost sight of Ben. When I turned back to look for him it was clear that he was no longer on the ward.

I immediately told the nurse in charge and expected her to at least alert your security and thought she might even assist in a search, however, she was obviously not interested and told me not to worry, as she was certain Ben would make his own way back to the ward.

I immediately panicked and searched without success only returning to the ward some fifteen minutes later by now frantic with worry. I was relieved when I saw an unknown member of the public walking back towards the ward with Ben. He told me he had found Ben outside as he was just leaving the entrance.

Anything could have happened to Ben if it had not been for the member of the public and I feel totally let down by your hospital and staff.

Jane Farrow

Jane Farrow

Jane Farrow's first line:

My son went missing in your hospital and no one could be bothered to help, anything could have happened to him, this can't be right can it?

Example Exercise 2

Interactive exercise

Smith

Candidate information

In this exercise there are two pages of information.

1   A general report from Hilary Dornan, the First Contact Manager.

2   A visitor's information report.

General report

From:	Hilary Dornan, First Contact Manager
To:	Candidate, First Contact Officer
Date:	Yesterday evening
Subject:	Edgar Smith

Over the last 12 months there has been an influx of migrant workers to the area, in response to the need for construction workers to assist in the continued development of the town.

Many of these workers have come, quite understandably with their families, but due to language and cultural issues some have not accessed the health care they require and this has led, on occasions, to some migrants having more complicated or prolonged health issues than would have been necessary had an early health intervention been made.

To try to prevent this happening again an open evening was planned for last evening commencing at 6.30 p.m. for migrants and this was advertised in the local press and support groups. The hospital grossly underestimated the numbers who were to attend and this resulted in a delay to the start of the meeting due to the car parks becoming full along with a change of venue to accommodate the large numbers. As the migrants changed venue this caused corridors around the hospital to become overcrowded although thankfully no one was hurt because of this.

It was probably as a result of this that Edgar Smith was seriously delayed in getting to visit his wife who is in the hospital following a routine operation.

As a result of the delays Mr Smith was only able to see his wife for 20 minutes rather than the full hour, and in the circumstances it is understandable that he was not happy.

I have arranged for you to meet with Edgar Smith to discuss what took place.

Hilary Dornan

Hilary Dornan
First Contact Manager

Visitors' information report

Person reporting issue/incident: Edgar Smith

Address: 31 Roselands
            Central Town
            CT3 1AH

Date information received: Yesterday evening at 8.30 p.m.

Yesterday evening I visited your hospital to see my wife, I was particularly anxious as I had been away on business so had not seen her for two days.

I had allowed more than enough time to ensure I was on time, however I found that I was unable to park anywhere near the hospital and then had difficulties getting through the masses of foreigners who were hanging around your corridors waiting for some opening evening to start. Apparently you were putting this on for them to ensure they could get access to all our health care services easily.

As a result of this I did not get to my wife until 7.40, but was required to leave at the end of the session at 8 p.m. despite my protests to the matron. I think it is totally unacceptable that having paid my taxes for all these years I can't even get a proper opportunity to see my wife but at the same time you are wasting money on open evenings. I trust such things will not happen again in the future,

Yours,

Edgar Smith

Edgar Smith's first line:

You're putting on special evenings for these foreigners and I can't even get to see my wife for an hour, it's disgraceful I want something done.

TOP TIPS

- Read the information you are provided with in the preparation phase slowly and carefully.
- Make notes in list form that will act as memory joggers when you meet the role actor in part two of the exercise.
- Take your notes from the preparation phase with you and use them.
- Use the information you are given in the activity room to check the details, if necessary.
- Do not make assumptions based on the role actor's racial origin or sex.
- Listen to the role actor and respond to what he or she says.
- Do not write during the 90-second interval or when you meet the role actor.
- Give the role actor time to say his or her opening line when you enter the room.
- Use open rather than closed questions.
- If you finish before the end of the five minutes, recap on what you have asked the role actor, his or her responses and the agreed actions.

INDIVIDUAL LEARNING POINTS

_____

_____

_____

_____

_____

_____

_____

_____

_____

Chapter 6
Written Exercises

Introduction

A key part of a police officer's role is to record information and, subsequently, to write up this information in such documents as statements of evidence. These documents must be both legible and understandable. The written tests assess your basic writing skills rather than your knowledge of the finer points of English grammar. The assessors are looking for candidates who can produce written information that is legible, accurate and easy to understand.

The number of written exercises

There are two written exercises. In both you must read and understand some information and then provide a written response to this information, as instructed in the exercise.

Briefing

Before the exercises, you will be fully briefed as to what is expected of you. You will be told where you should record your candidate number, the time limit for each exercise and how the exercises are conducted. You will also be told what to do if you make a mistake. As with the other briefings, to make sure you understand them fully, you will be asked to read certain instructions while the invigilator reads them out aloud.

Outline of a written exercise

The written exercises are very similar to the interactive exercises, the main difference being that, in the written exercises, you write your response down rather than speak it. Each written exercise has a time limit of 20 minutes, which includes time for you to read the exercise.

At the start of each exercise you will be provided with the exercise itself, pens and a form on which to write your response. Extra sheets are available if you run out of space on the form, and you will be provided with paper on which you can make rough notes.

How to approach the written exercises

Read through the exercise and think carefully about the task you have been set. Do not rush this: a few extra minutes spent considering the exercise and task will save you time later.

You write your response using the same job role you used for the interactive exercises. As before, if you need a policy from the information pack, this will be provided. Again, it is important you read and understand the information sent to you prior to attending for assessment. This should make reading the policies at the Assessment Centre a memory jog rather than having to understand them from scratch.

Be very clear as to what you must provide in your response. Before you write your final answer, make a list of all those things you want to mention. This will help you to focus on the key points you must cover.

TASK 1

Read the example written exercise, but do not complete the blank general report form until you have done Task 2 and read Task 3.

Written exercise

'Parking Enforcement'

Candidate information

In this exercise there are four pages of pre-information.

1. A general report from Hilary Dornan, the First Contact Manager.

2. A graph showing the increasing number of complaints regarding the issue of parking fixed penalty notices.

3. A copy of the First Contact Officer's job description.

4. A copy of the parking policy.

You are required to provide a written response. (A blank report form is provided below for your answer.)

Central Hospital Trust

General report

From: Hilary Dornan, First Contact Manager
To: Candidate, First Contact Officer
Date: Two days ago
Subject: Increasing number of complaints regarding the issue of fixed penalty
notices against drivers parking in unauthorised parking areas.

Please find attached a graph that shows the increasing number of complaints regarding the receipt of fixed penalty notices. Previously complaints have been very rare.

The parking manager and his staff are tasked to ensure roads on the hospital grounds are kept free from obstruction to ensure easy access for ambulances. Part of the process for doing this is enforcement of parking prohibitions through the issue of enforceable fixed penalty notices.

The increase in complaints has coincided with the main entrance for patients being moved away from the main car park by some distance and currently there is no drop-off zone nearby. Currently approximately one in five tickets leads to a complaint. Most complainants accept fully that, in hindsight, they had parked in contravention of the displayed signs but all say it was for a very short period while they assisted an elderly or infirm patient to the hospital before returning to their cars and parking them in appropriate spaces.

Please consider the situation and report on this, outlining the issues and potential solutions as the current situation is damaging the reputation of the hospital locally and taking increasing lengths of time to resolve the complaints.

Hilary Dornan

Hilary Dornan
First Contact Manager

Complaints regarding receipt of parking fixed penalty notices

Central Hospital Trust

First Contact Officer's job description

First Contact Officers work in fixed areas at the entrances to all wards and departments. When appropriate they will visit areas of the hospital, as directed, to deal with non-medical issues and concerns.

Time away from the identified fixed areas should be kept to a minimum, as these are the advertised contact points for patients, visitors and staff.

They report to the First Contact Manager and their duty times will be agreed to ensure cover between 8.00 a.m. and 10.00 p.m.

Their main responsibilities are as follows.

- Act as a point of contact for all non-medical issues concerning patients and visitors.

- Receive, inquire into and resolve any non-medical problems concerning staff, patients and visitors.

- Complete written reports on all matters reported to them.

- Ensure the Patient Confidentiality Policy is adhered to and explained fully to patients and visitors when required. They will also be available to give staff advice on this issue.

- Enforce, as required, the no-smoking policy among staff, patients and visitors.

- Give advice to staff, patients and visitors on the Equality Policy.

- Assist the First Contact Manager in ensuring all Trust policies and procedures are complied with.

- Work with the parking and shop managers regarding security and the provision of services.

- Provide assistance, as required, following the activation of fire or security alarms.

Central Hospital Trust

Parking Policy

Parking in the hospital environment is managed and enforced by an independent management company. This is for staff, patients and visitors' private vehicles.

Staff are able to park free of charge providing vehicles are correctly parked in staff-designated zones and vehicles are displaying the appropriate hospital vehicle passes.

All drivers of private vehicles are required to pay the charges for parking as indicated on the prominently displayed boards at the entrance to each car park.

The only exception to this are the 20-minute zones near to the entrances of each ward that allow for free short-term parking for the 'dropping off' and 'picking up' of patients.

Failure to park correctly or pay appropriate charges can lead to the award of a fixed penalty charge against the driver by the management company, who can subsequently enforce any non-payment as a civil debt.

Central Hospital Trust

General report

From: Candidate, First Contact Officer
To: Hilary Dornan, First Contact Manager
Date: Today's date

_____

_____

_____

_____

_____

_____

_____

_____

_____

_____

_____

_____

_____

_____

_____

_____

_____

_____

TASK 2

When you are clear about what you have been asked to do, write in list form what you think should be included in your written response. Make sure you outline the issues and the potential solutions. As with the notes you make for the interactive exercises, you are the only person who will read these, so they do not have to be written in full. Single words will often be enough. Now compare your list with the one below.

Example issues

- The increase in complaints has coincided with the move of the hospital entrance away from the main car park.

- The increased numbers of complaints against the numbers of tickets issued.

- The current month-on-month increases.

- Damage to the hospital's reputation and the time taken in resolving the complaints.

Review the complaints to try and ascertain the following.

- Why cars had been parked contrary to the signs displayed.

- If drivers knew they were parking in contravention of the parking notices.

- The reasons for complaints to see if there is an emerging pattern to the complaints.

Review the parking enforcement to ascertain the following.

- Are the current no parking signs clear?

- Is there a particular pattern to when the fixed penalty notices are being issued?

- Whether all parking operatives are issuing similar numbers of fixed penalty notices.

In addition a visit should be made to the parking manager to review any changes:

- to parking regulations or policies over the last four months;

- to parking enforcement over the same time period;

- of staff members over the same time period.

Example activities following the above actions.

- Review current parking restrictions in consultation with the parking manager, in light of the change to the main entrance, to have a set-down zone for patients with an agreed time period for which cars can be left in the zone free of charge, to allow patients to be taken into the hospital.

- All parking staff and first contact officers to be briefed as to any changes.

- Provide publicity and clear signs to ensure the public are aware of any parking enforcement.

- Provide publicity and clear signs to ensure the public are fully aware of drop-off zones.

TASK 3

Using your list to guide you, write your full written response on the form provided. Do this within the 20 minutes you will be allocated when you do these exercises at the Assessment Centre.

Your written response should be in complete sentences and paragraphs. You can, however, use lists within this structure, if appropriate. Apart from this, there is no set way you should present your answers.

If you make a mistake or want any part of your response to be ignored, simply put a diagonal line through it. You should also put a diagonal line through your planning list, even if this is on a separate sheet. Anything you write at the Assessment Centre will be collected and anything not crossed through will be marked.

How the written exercises are assessed

The marking scheme is very similar to that for the interactive exercises. The assessor will look at your response to see whether you have included the identified behaviours on his or her checklist, and he or she will also consider how well you have tackled these.

For example, the fact that Carnell's Music has made more calls for assistance than any other retail outlet would be identified as a behaviour. Stating that Carnell's Music *appears* to have made more calls than any other outlet would score, but not very well. Stating that the number of calls from Carnell's Music was *disproportionate* because they had made 15 calls while the next highest was only 4, on the other hand, would be a very strong way of scoring.

In addition to the behaviours, your written English is also assessed for common errors covering such issues as the following.

- Can it be read?
- Is it structured in sentence and paragraph form?
- Are words spelt incorrectly?
- Are the correct words used?
- Are there full stops at the end of sentences, followed by capitals?
- Are words missed out of sentences?
- Misuse of plurals.

Before you continue, assess your report using the above as a marking guide. If you are uncertain about how to do this, ask someone else to look at it for you.

At the Assessment Centre, only use words you know the meaning of. For example: 'Their are four outlets that have made calls for assistance.' You are unsure whether 'their' should be 'there'. If this is the case, think of an alternative way of saying the same thing (for example, 'four outlets have made calls for assistance'). Also make sure that you only use words you can spell correctly.

Use easy-to-understand sentences, and make sure your writing is legible. If you need to develop your skills in this area, write short accounts of everyday happenings (such as a day at work) and ask someone who has the appropriate skills to read them. Ask this person to use the list above as a marking guide.

To work out a candidate's grade for his or her standard of written English, the assessor adds up the number of mistakes the candidate has made in his or her response. This number is compared with a grid that shows which grade is awarded for that number of mistakes. As in the other exercises, the grade range is A–D.

Time

As mentioned above, you have 20 minutes to complete each written exercise. As well as there being a clock in the room, you will be told when there are five minutes remaining, then one minute remaining.

Don't worry if you do not finish: don't sacrifice quality for speed. If your response cannot be read, it cannot be scored. Illegible answers will be counted as mistakes, and this will affect your grade. If you do finish before the end, use this time to check your work thoroughly.

GENERAL ASSUMPTION

The more you write in the 20 minutes, the better your score.

FACT

Quantity is not a key factor in the scoring. While you want to achieve as many of the behaviours on the assessment checklist as possible, the quality of your writing is also important. You can score a lot of things on the checklist badly or a few things well and still achieve a similar overall grade. The key to success is reducing errors to the minimum or eradicating them completely.

Practise beforehand so that you know roughly how much writing you can produce within a 20-minute period. This practice will also ensure that you include all the key elements in your response.

TOP TIPS

- Identify clearly what is required in the written response to each exercise.
- Before you begin your response, make a list to structure the key elements of your answer.
- Write legibly.
- Only use words you can spell.
- Only use words you know the meaning of.
- Write simple sentences.
- Use full stops at the end of sentences and capital letters at the beginning of sentences.
- Use paragraphs to structure your answer.
- Cross out any writing you do not want marked.
- Use the 20 minutes to the full.

INDIVIDUAL LEARNING POINTS

_____

_____

_____

_____

_____

_____

_____

_____

_____

Chapter 7
Interviews

Introduction

Assessment Centre interviews have been designed very carefully and they are not like typical job interviews. They have been designed so that every candidate is given the same information and questions and, therefore, the same opportunity to demonstrate his or her skills and abilities.

Although water should be available during the interview, many of the pleasantries that are used to start a typical job interview will not be present. Be ready for this, and do not let it put you off.

The questions

You will be asked to talk about the ways you have used your abilities in the past – past behaviour is a good indicator of future performance. For example, a typical question would be: 'Please tell me about an occasion when you worked as part of a team to complete a goal or task.'

Another type of question is to give you a set of circumstances and to ask you what you would do in that situation. For example: 'You are working with someone who you know is lying about his or her part in an incident in order to absolve him or herself of any responsibility, when actually he or she is to blame. What would you do?'

Whatever form of question is used, the issues to consider when answering them are the same, and it is these issues that are discussed in this chapter.

GENERAL ASSUMPTION

The questions will be based on police topics or issues.

> **FACT**
>
> No questions will be based on police experiences or scenarios. The questions concern life in general, and you can answer them using your work, volunteer, social or educational experiences. This should give you every opportunity to reply to the questions in your own way. No particular experiences are considered more worthy than others. For example, an answer outlining a school or college experience would be assessed in the same way as one outlining a work-based activity. What is important is the answer's content: the skills a police officer needs can be transferred from non-police experiences and subsequently developed.

Important note: Some police forces hold additional interviews after the candidates have completed the Assessment Centre successfully. If the force you have applied to holds such interviews, contact the force for advice and assistance on the content and style of the interviews.

Your role during the interview

Unlike the interactive and written exercises, during the interview you are expected to be yourself: you are not required to play a role. It is important that, no matter what questions you are asked, you provide full and honest answers.

Do not take anything for granted. The questioner can only score what he or she hears. If it is not said, it cannot be scored – do not presume that the questioner will assume the obvious. If appropriate, you should explain your thought processes as well as your actions.

Briefing

Before the interview, you will be given a short briefing that outlines which room your interview will take place in and the structure it will follow. When you arrive in the interview room, the interviewer will read from a card an outline of what will happen during the interview. He or she will explain that you will be asked a series of questions and that the maximum time allowed to answer each question is five minutes. This is timed using a stopwatch.

He or she will also explain that, if you answer in less than five minutes, you will move on to the next question. Any time not used in one question, however, cannot be added to the next: the maximum time for each of the four questions is always five minutes.

If you finish the interview early, you will usually be told to remain in the interview room until the other candidates have finished. This is because most Assessment Centres do not have a holding room in which you could wait until the others finish. Should this happen, do not attempt to engage the interviewer in conversation – just sit quietly until you are told you may leave.

The structure of the interview

Normally, the only people in the room will be the interviewer and yourself. At the start of each five minutes, the interviewer states which competency area is being considered before he or she asks you the question. When you answer the question, the interviewer will assess your response.

Sometimes a third person may be present. This is to ensure that the questions are being asked and assessed appropriately. Should this happen, the reasons why this third person is there will be explained to you.

The interviewer will also have a number of prompts he or she can use to ask you to explain, or expand on your answers. If a question concerned team working, for example, a prompt might be as follows: 'Tell me what your role was in the team.' This prompt would encourage you to explain more about what you did in the team.

There may be five or six prompts for each question. If the interviewer does not need to use a particular prompt, he or she will not ask it. For example, if a candidate included a great deal of detail in his or her reply to the original team-working question (about what the team did, his or her role in it and how his or her role impacted on the rest of the team), asking the candidate what role he or she played in the team would not be appropriate.

Remember, the interviewers can only use the prescribed prompts, and they use them to help you achieve the best possible scores you can. Prompts are not there to try to catch you out.

You will be told at the start of the interview how many questions will be asked and that each question may have additional prompts. Your information pack will tell you how many questions you will be asked (usually four) and the competency area each question will cover.

One question, one competency

It has been mentioned on more than one occasion in this book that you should have a thorough understanding of what each competency area covers. This knowledge will help you to keep your answers focused on the appropriate indicators within that area.

While the interviewer will be concerned mainly with the stated competency area for each question, he or she will also assess your oral communication skills and Respect for Race and Diversity. Your oral communication skills are scored in the same way as they are for the interactive exercises. Any evidence you may give relating to other competency areas will not be assessed.

Before you attend for assessment, consider your past experiences and how you could use these to answer the questions. Practise answering possible questions, keeping your eye on the competency areas listed in **Appendix A**.

TASK 1

Interview question

Below is a question with space for you to write the answer you would give in the interview. (If you prefer, ask someone to read the question to you and to note down your reply.) Also below are example prompts that could be used to encourage you to explain or develop your answers.

This question is in the competency area Team Working.

Please tell me about a time when you have worked as part of a team to complete a goal or task.

Prompt 1: Tell me what your role in the team was.

Prompt 2: Outline exactly what you did.

Prompt 3: Tell me how you helped or supported others in the team.

Prompt 4: How did you assist the team to get over any difficulties or obstructions in achieving the goal or task?

TASK 1

Prompt 5: What was the final outcome with regards to achieving the goal or task?

Prompt 6: Is there anything else you wish to add in response to this question?

When you have completed this task, see how your answer compares with the Team Working competency area and its positive indicators. The assessor's checklist may not include all the positive indicators but it will include those appropriate to the question. Remember to consider not only which part of your answer relates to which indicators but also whether your answer provides strong or weak evidence.

Example answer

An answer to prompt 3 may be as follows: 'Before starting the task we checked that everyone had the skills to do their part of the task and, if they didn't, we either arranged training or we moved them on to other roles.' This part of the answer covers the following indicators.

- Makes time to get to know people.
- Co-operates with and supports others.
- Offers to help other people.
- Develops mutual trust and confidence in others.

The assessor would then make a decision about the strength of the answer. While it has merits, it only explains what was done at the start of the process. A fuller answer would go on to explain how support was provided throughout the activity. The answer is further weakened because the assessor would not be clear as to what the candidate actually did, as opposed to the team as a whole.

The assessor adds up how many indicators on his or her checklist for that question have been achieved and then decides how well each was done. A final grade for that question is then awarded.

Further example questions

Below are some further interview questions for you to consider. You should repeat Task 1 for each of the questions. This could well assist you by having to the forefront of your mind examples that can be used and adapted during the assessment centre. It will also increase your knowledge of the content of the competency areas.

1. This question relates to the competency area Problem Solving
   Please tell me about a problem you have previously resolved.
   If required consider the following prompts.
   a) Why did you choose to solve that problem?
   b) Tell me about how you went about solving the problem?
   c) What factors did you take into account in solving the problem?
   d) Did you consider alternatives to the solution you adopted?
   e) How did you choose the solution you adopted?
   f) How did you decide the problem had been successfully resolved?
   g) Is there anything else you wish to add in response to this question?

2. This question relates to the competency area Personal Responsibility
   Please tell me about a time when you took responsibility to ensure something was done when others chose to ignore the situation.
   If required consider the following prompts.
   a) Why did you decide to take action?
   b) What do you think caused others to ignore the situation?
   c) What did you consider before deciding to act?
   d) What actions did you take?
   e) What was the outcome of the actions you took?
   f) Is there anything else you wish to add in response to this question?

3. This question relates to the competency area Community and Customer Focus
   Please tell me about a time when you were involved in providing a service to an individual, group or the general public.
   If required consider the following prompts.
   a) How was the need for the service developed/decided upon?
   b) What was the service provided?
   c) What actions did you take to ensure that the service provided was appropriate?
   d) How did you judge if the service provided was well received?
   e) Is there anything else you wish to add in response to this question?

4. This question relates to the competency area Effective Communication
   Please tell me about a time when you have changed or amended your communication in order to ensure that your communication was as clear as possible.
   If required consider the following prompts.
   a) What were you trying to communicate?
   b) What caused you to think a change/amendment to the communication method was necessary?

c) What did you consider before changing/amending your communication?

d) What were the reasons you changed/amended your communication?

e) What were the changes you made in your communication?

f) How did you judge whether the new communication method was clearer than the original method?

g) Is there anything else you wish to add in response to this question?

Using the five minutes to best effect

Remember, you can score very well without saying everything you want to say about a particular question, so don't worry if you are stopped because the five minutes is up. If you are asked a question for which you cannot think of an answer, the interviewer will suggest you return to that question after you have answered the others. You will not be marked down for this, but neither will you be granted extra time for the same question being asked twice.

If you finish before the end of the five minutes, the questioner will always ask you a general prompt, similar to number 6 above. While you should not talk just for the sake of talking, you can only score when you are talking. The five minutes is yours and, if you have the time, it is worth recapping on your answers. There are two reasons for this.

- Working through an answer from the beginning to the conclusion can often prompt you to expand on, or explain part of your answer more fully.

- By repeating an answer you may score the same area again, but if you use different words or expand your answer, you may score that area more strongly than before. Your strongest answer is always used when calculating your final grade. Similarly, if you touch on the same area again and again, as long as each part of your answer adds to the evidence, this will be taken into consideration when the strength of your answer is assessed.

How the interview scores are used

The scores for each question are added to the scores you achieve for the same competency areas in the other exercises. This produces your total for that competency area. For example, one of the interview questions covered Community and Customer Focus. This was also covered in two interactive and one written exercise. These four scores are added together to produce your final score for this competency area. This score is then added to your overall assessment.

TOP TIPS

- Be prepared for a very structured interview.
- Before attending the Assessment Centre, consider in detail the competency areas the questions will be based on.
- Prepare answers in your mind that you may be able to use in the interview.
- Keep your answers focused on the stated competency area.
- Listen carefully to prompts and expand on, or add to your answer accordingly.
- Make sure you explain your involvement when you are asked about your previous experiences.
- Use your full five minutes for each question.
- Should you finish early, recap on your answer.

INDIVIDUAL LEARNING POINTS

_____

_____

_____

_____

_____

_____

_____

_____

_____

Chapter 8
Respect for Race and Diversity

Introduction

The task in **Chapter 2** will have shown you what this competency area is all about, but it is worth repeating here. Respect for Race and Diversity means to consider and show respect for the opinions, circumstances and feelings of colleagues and members of the public, no matter what their position, background, circumstances, status or appearance.

To achieve this competency area you must understand other people's views and take these into account. You must also be tactful and diplomatic when dealing with people, treating them with dignity and respect at all times. You must understand and be sensitive to social, cultural and racial differences. Although race and diversity are included in this area, it is not restricted to certain groups only. It is worth, therefore, revisiting **Appendix A** to review both the positive and negative indicators.

Why this area is important

Many inquiries and reports into the police service have shown that policing breaks down when the community it serves feels alienated from the police and their actions. The police service is built on the concept of 'policing by consent'. This concept is crucial if the public are to support the police in maintaining a safe and secure society.

The most recent and far-reaching investigation into how policing is conducted was the Stephen Lawrence Inquiry. This inquiry introduced the term 'institutional racism'. In simple terms, this means having policies and procedures – official or otherwise – that disadvantage certain racial or ethnic groups. The report of this inquiry had a dramatic impact on the police service, and it is one of the reasons why the National Police Recruit Assessment Process was introduced.

The term 'institutional racism' can be broadened to include all sectors of society. Take, for example, a group of 'hoodies' standing at a street corner talking. Many people would assume that they are up to no good. Should police officers assume this, it would considerably affect any exchanges the police officers and youths had.

TASK 1

'Institutional racism'

Local residents have complained about problems they have had with teenagers in their neighbourhood. You are one of two police officers who have been asked to patrol this area. You see a group of six youths standing on a street corner with hoods covering their heads and faces. They appear to turn away from you. Remember, you are there because of complaints from local residents, and these residents will be watching what you do.

Before continuing, list below the actions you would consider in these circumstances.

Having done this, review your responses against the indicators for this competency area (see **Appendix A**). First, identify those intended behaviours that would be considered positive. Now identify those that would be considered negative. (Remember, try to develop your skills so that only positive behaviours are observed during your assessment.)

Your opening comments to the group could dramatically affect their perception of the police: they may well have nothing to hide and are just standing there, talking. They only turned away because of their previous bad interactions with police officers. From their point of view they have done nothing wrong, and they are being picked on simply because of their dress code.

Should you just tell them bluntly to move on or they will be arrested, it would be easy to see why they have issues with the police. It would be much better if you told the group why you were in the area, mentioned the local residents' concerns and discussed with them why they congregate on street corners, etc.

Obviously, if it became apparent that the group were involved in anti-social or otherwise unlawful behaviour, then the exchange would be different. However, there is still a requirement even under these circumstances to treat people, as far as possible, with dignity and respect.

GENERAL ASSUMPTION

When 'older' people complain about teenagers, the 'older' people must be in the right and the teenagers in the wrong.

FACT

This may or may not be the case. If you are presented with a scenario like this at the Assessment Centre, consider the facts you have been given: what is fact and what is assumption?

For example, a group of youths have been seen hanging around an area, and this has been recorded on CCTV cameras. The next morning, there is graffiti on the walls in this area. The local residents are up in arms and are convinced these youths caused the damage.

From the information you have been given, this is an assumption. If at the Assessment Centre you were asked to speak to a local resident, first establish what is fact and what is assumption. If there is no evidence that the youths were responsible, you should make it clear that, while such damage is unacceptable, inquiries will have to be made to establish who was responsible and that action will be taken to prevent it from happening again.

Many candidates have opinions similar to the following.

● Groups of youths cannot be trusted.

● Youths wearing hoods have something to hide.

● The youth of today have little respect for property or people.

● If a group of youths is in an area and something happens, then they must be responsible.

Candidates with opinions such as these side easily with role actors who are playing the part of victims. Such candidates often say 'they shouldn't be allowed to wear hoods' or 'that behaviour is typical of young people today'. Comments like this do not display many of the positive indicators for Respect for Race and Diversity. They do not demonstrate:

● considering the issue from the teenagers' point of view;

● treating them with dignity and respect;

● tolerance;

● respect for their needs;

● understanding; or

● respect for their values as these fall within what is lawful.

At the Assessment Centre you must show appropriate respect to all groups at all times, even if a group is not physically present. Do not express commonly held, stereotypical views.

How the area is scored

As mentioned elsewhere in this book, Respect for Race and Diversity is assessed all the time you are at the Assessment Centre – and this includes arriving at or leaving the centre. For example, a candidate is seen to hit another car when he is reversing out of the car park at the end of the Assessment Centre. Instead of reporting this, he drives off. This candidate's behaviour demonstrates the following.

- He has clearly not shown respect for the circumstances and feelings of his colleagues.

- He has not treated the other car-owner with respect.

- He has not identified and respected other people's values as these fall within what is lawful.

- He has not been open and honest.

- He has not considered the other car-owner's feelings.

- He has made the situation worse with his inappropriate behaviour.

There are Respect for Race and Diversity evidence sheets to record inappropriate behaviour such as this. Anyone in the assessment team who witnesses such behaviour is required to record what he or she saw or heard on these sheets. He or she should describe – in as much detail as possible – what took place, using the candidate's own words if this is appropriate. Any other team members who witnessed the incident will also sign the sheet to confirm that they, too, observed this behaviour.

A panel will then review this sheet. If the candidate had been successful at the Assessment Centre, it would be up to the panel to make the decision as to the candidate's suitability for appointment.

If inappropriate behaviour is displayed during the interactive exercises, written exercises or interview, this will be scored on the relevant assessment sheet under the competency area Respect for Race and Diversity. The observed behaviour will also be recorded on the Respect for Race and Diversity evidence sheet. The grade normally awarded under such circumstances would be a D. The Assessment Centre manager and the panel will review this score, bearing in mind the evidence recorded on the sheet. If they uphold the D then, no matter what else the candidate has scored, he or she will fail the Assessment Centre.

It is impossible to give a list of comments that would be deemed inappropriate, but if candidates express views that are sexist, racist or homophobic, then, quite rightly, they would be unsuccessful. You should, therefore, think about this area carefully. Candidates who hold such views should not consider a career in the police service: police officers must remain impartial at all times, even when their own values would naturally cause them to be sympathetic to one view rather than another.

Interview questions

It is likely that one of the interview questions will be based on this competency area. If this is the case, you will be notified in advance via your information pack. It is worthwhile preparing yourself for such a question because this will give you the opportunity to think about your own values and behaviours carefully and honestly, and to compare these with the positive and negative indicators. It will also mean you will have examples ready for when you are questioned.

An example question for Respect for Race and Diversity is as follows: 'Please tell me about a time when you've amended your behaviour or language to take into account another person's views or values.' Remember, your answers do not have to relate just to race and diversity but may include any differences in society. Below are a few examples.

- Not using the expression 'Christ' because you work with Christians.

- When organising a Christmas party, you ensure that non-alcoholic drinks are available.

- When on holiday, you change what you wear to conform with local customs or requirements (i.e. not going topless).

- Introducing flexi-time to allow people with childcare commitments to achieve a work–life balance.

- Even though you are permitted to play a radio quietly at work, you only play it when your boss is not there because she does not like people playing radios.

- Not mowing your lawn until mid-afternoon because your neighbour works nights and sleeps in the morning.

When answering, explain the differences between your own views and those of the other party, then describe how you considered and took into account their views and then amended your behaviour in the light of these differences.

The follow-up questions the interviewer could use may include the following.

- How did you become aware of this issue or problem?

- What did you consider before amending your thoughts or actions?

- What did you do about it?

- How do you feel about the other party's position?

- What was the resolution?

Remember, if there is time remaining you will be asked if you have anything further to add to your answer. Should you have time remaining in the five minutes use it to recap your answer.

TOP TIPS

- Study the positive and negative indicators for Respect for Race and Diversity.

- Remember that Respect for Race and Diversity relates to all differences in society.

- Use appropriate behaviour and language at all times.

- Deal with facts – do not make assumptions.

- During the exercises and tests, respect all the parties, even if they are not physically present.

- Do not stereotype.

- Remember, you are being observed even when you are not under formal assessment conditions.

- Bear in mind the positive indicators when you answer the Respect for Race and Diversity interview question.

INDIVIDUAL LEARNING POINTS

Chapter 9
Psychometric Tests

Introduction

A psychometric test is simply a way of measuring your mental abilities. There are two psychometric tests – one measures your numerical reasoning and the other your verbal logical reasoning. These tests are often referred to as PIRT (Police Initial Recruit Tests).

Numerical Reasoning Test

In this test you read a short scenario that contains some facts and figures. You are then presented with a question and four possible answers to this question. You must decide which one of the four answers is correct. You are not allowed to use calculators in this test but you can use rough paper to work out which is the correct answer. (Sample questions and answer sheets are given in this chapter.)

Verbal Logical Reasoning Test

This test requires you to read a series of statements and then to consider a list of conclusions based on these statements. When you have studied the conclusions, you have to decide whether, from what you have read in the statements, each one is 'true', 'false' or 'impossible to say' (i.e. neither true nor false). (Sample questions and answer sheets are given in this chapter.)

Time allowed and number of questions

The numerical reasoning test lasts 12 minutes and contains 25 questions. The verbal reasoning test lasts 25 minutes and contains 31 questions.

How the tests are administered

Both tests are usually conducted under formal examination conditions. While the number of candidates sitting the tests at any one time will be restricted by the size of the room available, the maximum number is normally 32. You will be told before each test how many questions it contains and how much time you have to complete it. You are then asked to do a few practice questions.

Following the completion of the practice questions, the administrator will go through the questions with you, explaining which are the correct answers and why.

Rules

After writing your name and candidate number on the answer sheet, you complete the practice questions, as mentioned above. You must not mark the question paper in any way as these will be reused. If you are given a question paper that has a previous candidate's working-outs on it, ignore these: put down what you consider to be the correct answer.

While there will be a clock in the room, you should monitor the time yourself. If you lay a wristwatch on your table, this will save you constantly looking up at the clock. No warnings are given as to how much time is left. When the time is up, the administrator will ask you to stop and will collect in the question and answer sheets.

GENERAL ASSUMPTION

It is better to give no answers than to guess wildly.

FACT

There is no system of negative marking – only correct answers are taken into account. Therefore complete all the questions – do not leave any unanswered.

How to complete the tests

Use the practice questions to familiarise yourself with the correct way to mark the answer sheet. You must fill in the circle on the answer sheet that corresponds to the answer you think is correct. Make sure you are marking the correct question number. This is particularly important if you have passed over a question with the intention of answering it later.

Monitor the time you have available – work out how many questions you should have answered by a certain time. For example, after six minutes of the numerical test, approximately 13 questions should have been completed. If you do this you will give yourself the same amount of time to answer all the questions and will not have to rush towards the end.

Even though you should not simply guess the answers, neither should you leave any questions unanswered. If you only complete 75 per cent of the questions, you will not have scored anything in the remaining 25 per cent. This will dramatically reduce the score you could have achieved for that test.

A balance has to be struck between speed and accuracy. If you are stuck on a question, either leave it until the end (making sure you skip the appropriate space on the answer sheet) or choose what appears to be the most appropriate answer and then continue with the remaining questions. While the tests appear to have a lot of questions, most candidates do complete them within the time limit.

How the tests are scored

Depending on the total number of correct answers you achieve, you will be awarded either a grade A, B, C or D. Grade A is the top and grade D is the bottom.

Numerical Reasoning Test: Example

Below are some example questions for the Numerical Reasoning Test. Using the answer sheet provided, select which one of the four possible answers you consider to be correct. (A completed answer sheet can be found later in this chapter.)

1 A firm orders 50 reams of paper but only 10 reams arrive. What percentage of the order has been received?

A	B	C	D
5%	20%	36%	51%

2 An employee has flexible working hours. He must, however, remain at work for at least seven hours. If he arrives at 13.00 hours, what is the earliest time he can leave?

A	B	C	D
18.00 hrs	19.20 hrs	20.00 hrs	23.30 hrs

3 A man finds a wallet. In it are a £2 coin, a £10 note, a £5 note and three 1p coins. What is the total amount of cash in the wallet?

A	B	C	D
£12.20	£14.10	£24.30	£17.03

4 Trains leave a town for London at the rate of three per hour. How many trains are scheduled to leave for London between the hours of 8 am and 11 am?

A	B	C	D
2	9	15	20

5 A schoolboy has 230 sweets and is required to give 10% to his classmates. How many sweets is that?

A	B	C	D
100	84	46	23

6 A town has an average of 24 burglaries per month. How many burglaries would be expected in one year?

A	B	C	D
288	240	226	210

7 A school has ten classrooms, each with a maximum desk capacity of 31. Two classrooms have to be closed. What is the maximum number of desks the school can now have?

A	B	C	D
310	296	248	222

8 A shop has 100 watches for sale. None is sold, but 37 are stolen. How many remain for sale?

A	B	C	D
73	63	53	43

9 A car park has a maximum capacity of 200 cars. A set charge of £2 is made for each car parked. Each day 25% of the spaces are used. How much money is taken by the car park in one day?

A	B	C	D
£50	£125	£100	£75

10 A train leaves at 12.15 hours. The journey takes $3\frac{1}{2}$ hours. What time will the train arrive at its destination?

A	B	C	D
16.30	15.00	15.15	15.45

11 You are taking 40 children to a youth production at a theatre. As party leader your entrance fee is free but you have to pay for all the children at a cost of £2.85 per head. How much does it cost for all the children?

A	B	C	D
£58	£84	£101	£114

12 Two-fifths of a class of 25 pupils were girls. What percentage were boys?

A	B	C	D
20%	30%	45%	60%

13 An exam has a total of 20 questions, with a maximum of 4 marks available for each. If 100% was achieved, what would the actual mark awarded be?

A	B	C	D
100	80	60	40

14 To block a road to traffic 14 protesters must stand shoulder to shoulder. How many protesters would it take to block 8 roads at the same time?

A	B	C	D
86	94	112	118

15 A factory has 130 members of staff and 90% of the staff use the canteen daily. How many dinners must the chef prepare each day?

A	B	C	D
117	73	101	38

Numerical Reasoning Test: Example answer sheet

1	Ⓐ	Ⓑ	Ⓒ	Ⓓ
2	Ⓐ	Ⓑ	Ⓒ	Ⓓ
3	Ⓐ	Ⓑ	Ⓒ	Ⓓ
4	Ⓐ	Ⓑ	Ⓒ	Ⓓ
5	Ⓐ	Ⓑ	Ⓒ	Ⓓ
6	Ⓐ	Ⓑ	Ⓒ	Ⓓ
7	Ⓐ	Ⓑ	Ⓒ	Ⓓ
8	Ⓐ	Ⓑ	Ⓒ	Ⓓ
9	Ⓐ	Ⓑ	Ⓒ	Ⓓ
10	Ⓐ	Ⓑ	Ⓒ	Ⓓ
11	Ⓐ	Ⓑ	Ⓒ	Ⓓ
12	Ⓐ	Ⓑ	Ⓒ	Ⓓ
13	Ⓐ	Ⓑ	Ⓒ	Ⓓ
14	Ⓐ	Ⓑ	Ⓒ	Ⓓ
15	Ⓐ	Ⓑ	Ⓒ	Ⓓ

Numerical Reasoning Test:
Example completed answer sheet

1	Ⓐ	**Ⓑ**	Ⓒ	Ⓓ
2	Ⓐ	Ⓑ	**Ⓒ**	Ⓓ
3	Ⓐ	Ⓑ	Ⓒ	**Ⓓ**
4	Ⓐ	**Ⓑ**	Ⓒ	Ⓓ
5	Ⓐ	Ⓑ	Ⓒ	**Ⓓ**
6	**Ⓐ**	Ⓑ	Ⓒ	Ⓓ
7	Ⓐ	Ⓑ	**Ⓒ**	Ⓓ
8	Ⓐ	**Ⓑ**	Ⓒ	Ⓓ
9	Ⓐ	Ⓑ	**Ⓒ**	Ⓓ
10	Ⓐ	Ⓑ	Ⓒ	**Ⓓ**
11	Ⓐ	Ⓑ	Ⓒ	**Ⓓ**
12	Ⓐ	Ⓑ	Ⓒ	**Ⓓ**
13	Ⓐ	**Ⓑ**	Ⓒ	Ⓓ
14	Ⓐ	Ⓑ	**Ⓒ**	Ⓓ
15	**Ⓐ**	Ⓑ	Ⓒ	Ⓓ

Verbal Logical Reasoning Test: Example

Below are some example questions for the Verbal Logical Reasoning Test. To answer these, read the sentence outlining the situation and the known facts associated with this situation. Below this are a series of statements. Read these and decide for each one whether it is A) true, B) false or C) impossible to say. Record your answers on the answer sheet provided. (A completed answer sheet can be found later in this chapter.)

After five years with Central Sports, Jon Clough signed for Athletico United. The only facts known are:

- this was before the start of the new season;

- Jon signed for Athletico United at the end of his five-year contract with Central Sports;

- the fee was £10 million;

- the transaction involved money only;

- Jon has not played professionally for any other club;

- Jon signed with Central Sports on leaving school at the age of 18 and has had only one contract with them.

A – True

B – False

C – Impossible to say

1 As part of the transfer fee, another player went from Athletico United to Central Sports

2 Jon signed for Athletico United in August

3 This was Jon's fourth professional club

4 Jon is 29 years of age

5 Jon scored 84 goals while he was with Central Sports

> Minesh Mistri was murdered on the evening of 4th November. He was found dead in the village of Ecton. The only facts known are:
>
> - he was murdered by a single blow from a blunt instrument;
> - he left his home address in Northampton at 4.00 p.m. on that day;
> - his friend, Derek Smith, saw him alive at 3.00 p.m. on 4th November;
> - Minesh's car was found abandoned very near to the scene of the crime;
> - Minesh was of Asian origin;
> - he was murdered where his body was found.

A – True

B – False

C – Impossible to say

  6 The murder weapon was a knife

  7 The murder happened between 4.00 p.m. and midnight

  8 Minesh's car was found abandoned in Northampton

  9 Derek was the last person to see Minesh alive

10 Minesh was the victim of a racially motivated attack

> All types of businesses and work premises are equally likely to have staff that suffer a heart attack while at work. The only facts known are:
>
> - it affects all grades of staff equally;
> - employers with appropriately trained first aid staff on a business site have less fatalities of staff from heart attacks than other businesses;
> - people who have a heart attack should not be allowed to work any overtime when they return to work;
> - both genders and all ethnic origins are likely to suffer heart attacks at work;
> - no research regarding age as a factor has been undertaken at this time.

A – True

B – False

C – Impossible to say

11 Working overtime brings on a heart attack

12 Due to pressures senior managers are more likely to suffer a heart attack

13 People over 50 are more likely to suffer a heart attack

14 Staff from both factories and office environments are likely to have heart attacks

15 Staff who have heart attacks in jobs where first aid trained staff are readily available are more likely to live following a heart attack at work

Verbal Logical Reasoning Test:
Example answer sheet

1	Ⓐ	Ⓑ	Ⓒ
2	Ⓐ	Ⓑ	Ⓒ
3	Ⓐ	Ⓑ	Ⓒ
4	Ⓐ	Ⓑ	Ⓒ
5	Ⓐ	Ⓑ	Ⓒ
6	Ⓐ	Ⓓ	Ⓒ
7	Ⓐ	Ⓑ	Ⓒ
8	Ⓐ	Ⓑ	Ⓒ
9	Ⓐ	Ⓑ	Ⓒ
10	Ⓐ	Ⓑ	Ⓒ
11	Ⓐ	Ⓑ	Ⓒ
12	Ⓐ	Ⓑ	Ⓒ
13	Ⓐ	Ⓑ	Ⓒ
14	Ⓐ	Ⓑ	Ⓒ
15	Ⓐ	Ⓑ	Ⓒ

Verbal Logical Reasoning Test:
Example completed answer sheet

1	(A)	**(B)**	(C)
2	(A)	(B)	**(C)**
3	(A)	**(B)**	(C)
4	(A)	**(B)**	(C)
5	(A)	(B)	**(C)**
6	(A)	**(B)**	(C)
7	**(A)**	(B)	(C)
8	(A)	**(B)**	(C)
9	(A)	(B)	**(C)**
10	(A)	(B)	**(C)**
11	(A)	(B)	**(C)**
12	(A)	**(B)**	(C)
13	(A)	(B)	**(C)**
14	**(A)**	(B)	(C)
15	**(A)**	(B)	(C)

How to practise for the tests

Numerical Reasoning Test

Work on those areas you know you are weak in (for example, addition, subtraction, multiplication or division). Do you feel confident when using fractions and percentages? Do you understand the 24-hour clock? If you are unsure of any of these areas, ask someone reliable to help you with them.

Look at the questions you have just answered. Did you get the right answers? Did you identify quickly the maths required for each scenario? Some of these questions are given below (without the scenarios) as straightforward maths problems:

Questions 3 asks the following.

$$£2.00$$
$$+ £10.00$$
$$+ £5.00$$
$$+ £0.03$$

$$= £17.03$$

This makes the answer D.

Question 7 asks the following.

$$10 - 2 = 8$$
$$8 \times 31 = 248$$

This makes the answer C.

Question 8 asks the following.

$$100 - 37 = 63$$

This makes the answer B.

Question 9 asks the following.

$$25\% \times 200 = 50$$
$$50 \times 2 = 100$$

This makes the answer C.

Question 15 asks the following.

$$100\% - 90\% = 10\%$$
$$10\% \times 130 = 13$$
$$130 - 13 = 117$$

This makes the answer A.

If you were unsure how to solve any of the questions, try working them out again as simple maths problems (without the scenarios), as above.

Verbal Logical Reasoning Test

Were you able to decide quickly whether a statement was true, false or impossible to say? Below are a few example statements from the Verbal Logical Reasoning Test you have just completed with explanations as to why they are true, false or impossible to say.

Question 1 asks whether, as part of the transfer fee, another player went from Athletico United to Central Sports. You know from points 3 and 4 that the fee was £10 million but that the transaction involved money only. From these facts you can deduce that another player did not go to Central Sports as part of the fee. Hence the answer is B (false).

Question 2 asks whether Jon signed for Athletico United in August. We know Jon signed before the new season started, but we do not know when it commenced. It may have been August but, equally, it may well not have been. Therefore the answer is C (impossible to say).

Question 7 asks whether the murder happened between 4.00 p.m. and midnight. We know Minesh left his home at 4.00 p.m. and was murdered during the evening. Therefore the answer is A (true).

Question 8 asks whether Minesh's car was found abandoned in Northampton. We know that Minesh was murdered in Ecton and that his car was abandoned very near to the scene of the crime. From these facts we can deduce that his car was not found abandoned in Northampton. Therefore the answer is B (false).

Question 15 asks if people who suffer from heart attacks where first aid staff are present at work are more likely to live. We know that employers who have first aid trained staff on site have fewer fatalities to staff who have heart attacks at work. From this fact we can deduce if a trained first aid member of staff is present you are more likely to survive. Therefore the answer is A (true).

You can practise your skills of deduction by reading articles in newspapers and magazines, etc., particularly those that have editorial comments. Read the conclusions the writer of the article has reached and then consider the known facts. On the basis of these facts, are these conclusions true, false or impossible to say?

There are also many books available that may help you to prepare for both tests, and you may be able to find example tests on the Internet to practise with.

TOP TIPS

- Note carefully the time allowed for each test.
- Do not mark the question papers in any way.
- Manage your time during the test.
- Know roughly how many questions you must have answered by the mid-point of the test.
- Lay a wristwatch on the table beside you.
- Make sure you are marking the correct question number – particularly if you have passed over a question.
- Answer all the questions.
- Practise for both tests.

INDIVIDUAL LEARNING POINTS

_____

_____

_____

_____

_____

_____

_____

_____

_____

Chapter 10
After the Assessment Centre

Appeals

When you have completed the Assessment Centre, you are debriefed by the invigilators. The invigilators will tell you that you should raise any issues or concerns about the operation of the Assessment Centre before you leave the site. Any issues raised after the event will not be considered. You may discuss any concerns you have in private, away from the other candidates. You should not be afraid to highlight anything that may have adversely affected your performance, although it is rare for such things to happen.

Sometimes candidates say they knew a role actor or assessor personally and that this hindered their performance. While this is unfortunate, it is not grounds for appeal. Police officers sometimes have to deal with people they consider to be their friends, but they still have to handle such situations in their professional capacity as police officers. Everyday occurrences that may interrupt the running of the Assessment Centre, such as fire alarms, are normally remedied on the day by allowing the candidates extra time to finish. Such everyday occurrences are similarly not accepted as grounds for appeal.

Feedback on the assessment process

At the end of the assessment you will be given a questionnaire and a prepaid return envelope. This questionnaire asks you to comment on the appropriateness of the exercises and tests and to say whether you felt you were given the opportunity to demonstrate your skills and abilities to the full. The questionnaire is not part of the assessment process, and candidates are not monitored to see who completes and returns them. The comments the candidates make in the questionnaire are used to assess the effectiveness of the exercises and tests.

The assessors, role actors and members of the management team are also asked to comment on how well they felt the assessment went. The feedback obtained from all those involved consistently shows that the overwhelming majority believe the Assessment Centre is fair and appropriate (remember, some of these people are serving police officers).

Immediately after the Assessment Centre

The Assessment Centre is a demanding process, requiring concentration on your part over a long period of time. Take time to relax, therefore, once the assessment is over, particularly if you have to drive. If you have not eaten, have something to eat now. Also bear in mind that, even though the assessment has officially come to an end, you are still being observed and that any inappropriate behaviour will be recorded.

Fitness tests

The fitness tests are designed to test endurance and dynamic strength. This is because police officers are required to struggle or fight with individuals who resist arrest. This can involve pushing, pulling and/or generally grappling, sometimes over relatively sustained periods. Dependent on the police service to which you have applied these tests could happen before or after the Assessment Centre.

The dynamic strength of candidates is tested on a machine called the 'Dyno machine'. It requires candidates to perform five seated chest pushes and five seated back pulls. It is the average across the five pushes and the five pulls which gives the recorded scores.

The push can most easily be understood as a bench press and requires you to sit upright with your back against padding with your feet flat on the floor and your knees at 90 degrees. You grip the bar in line with the middle of your sternum and push. You are allowed three warm-up pushes before completing five tested pushes, with a gap of three seconds between each. The pull can most easily be understood as a rowing action. The process for the test is the same as followed for the pull. The standard is 35kg for the pull and 34kg for the push.

Endurance is tested through what is commonly known as the bleep test. This requires candidates to run up and down a 15-metre track in time with a sounding bleep, turning on the line at the end of the distance as the bleep sounds. If a candidate arrives at the line before the bleep sounds they are required to wait for the noise before continuing. The bleep between the two ends of the 15 metres gets progressively quicker as the test progresses. The speed required ranges from 4.9 m.p.h to 6.2 m.p.h. Candidates are required to continue until they can no longer keep up with the bleep. To pass this test, 35 shuttles are required and this equates to 525 metres but candidates should keep running until they can no longer keep up with the sound of the bleep.

A few forces have slightly amended endurance tests; however, all will be looking for a reasonable paced run lasting somewhere in the region of four minutes.

Obviously candidates should prepare to ensure that they can pass the fitness tests. Many police services will assist candidates in this. If this is offered then this is the best way of ensuring you are ready to take the tests. Exercising with free weights or resistance machines can increase dynamic strength, although care and advice must be taken to ensure this is done safely. Traditional-style press-ups are another way of improving upper body strength.

Endurance tests can be prepared for by commencing at a walking pace before increasing to a slow jog. Once you are satisfied that you have warmed up sufficiently try and run at a faster pace for approximately 10 minutes. This will be more advantageous than running at a slow pace for 20 minutes. You should aim to run at a pace that starts to affect your ability to talk normally. Do not just stop at the end of the ten minutes, move to a jog, followed by a slow walk, thereby allowing your body to return to its normal state before stopping.

Any exercise should be preceded and then followed by stretching exercises and professional advice should always be sought before commencing exercise. It cannot be stressed enough that a medical practitioner should always be consulted before beginning strenuous physical exercise.

In addition to the fitness tests candidates are also required to see a doctor/medical adviser to confirm their medical fitness to carry out duties as a constable. This usually comes right at the end of the recruit assessment process.

Police force interviews

Some police forces interview candidates after they have completed the Assessment Centre successfully. If the police force you have applied to holds such interviews, you will normally be notified of the time and location of your interview when you receive your assessment results.

These interviews are usually formal – you appear before a panel of three interviewers, one of whom is often a senior police officer. They last between 30 and 40 minutes and the questions you are asked normally concern that particular police force. Typical questions are as follows.

- Why do you want to be a police officer?

- What are the qualities you would bring to the office of constable?

- What are your hopes and aspirations for your chosen career?

- What are the main issues that concern this force?

- What are the objectives in the current policing plan?

You may also be asked questions about topical police or political issues, so it is a good idea to watch news programmes and to read the quality newspapers.

Because each force organises its own interviews, it is difficult to give specific advice about them. You should therefore ask the force how long it will last and who will be present. You could also inquire about the types of questions you will be asked – for example, whether about your previous experiences or whether about the force you have applied to. If they will ask you questions about the force itself, you should, as a minimum, obtain, read and understand that force's annual report.

Results from the Assessment Centre

The marks awarded to each candidate are sent to a central marking point. Although the exercises and tests are marked electronically, the marks are checked manually to make sure they are correct. The results are published within the next 14 days and they are sent to the relevant police forces. Each force then notifies its candidates in writing about their results.

You should not telephone in for your results as this slows the marking process down. It would also be unfair if candidates received their results at different times and through different methods.

Feedback

In addition to your results, you will also be sent detailed written feedback. Some candidates are often annoyed with their results and immediately telephone for more information. Should you be disappointed with your results, wait at least 24 hours before you read the feedback: take time first to consider how you performed at the Assessment Centre.

While there is nothing wrong in ringing for further information, remember that it is very unlikely the person you are speaking to was present at your assessment. Even if he or she was, it is highly improbable this person will remember you.

You will receive feedback on each exercise and test. This will outline which competency areas were being assessed, what grades you achieved and how well you performed in comparison with the other candidates. You are also sent a grid-like table with the competency areas down one side and the exercises across the top. This shows you the grades you were awarded for each exercise and test (remember, A is the top mark and D the bottom). This will tell you, at a glance, which competency areas you were strong in and which require work.

On seeing a poor mark in one competency area, some candidates often feel the assessment must have been flawed in some way. Should you feel this, revisit that competency area and look at both the positive and negative indicators. Use your own recollections of the Assessment Centre and the written feedback to reflect honestly on your performance: which of the positive indicators did you not provide strong evidence for while you were being assessed?

An example grid is as follows.

	Exercise 1 'Cox'	Exercise 2 'Exercise Name'	Exercise 3 'Exercise Name'	Exercise 4 'Exercise Name'
Respect for Race and Diversity	C	B	B	B
Team Working		B	B	C
Community and Customer Focus	D		C	D
Effective Communication	B	C	B	C
Problem Solving	A		A	A
Personal Responsibility		C	C	D
Resilience	C	B	C	B

This candidate scored well in the area of Problem Solving, but poorly in Community and Customer Focus. His or her score for oral communication skills would be included in the score for Effective Communication.

In addition to this grid, you will be sent an outline of the exercises that explains what the exercises were about, what competency areas were being assessed and what candidates did well and not so well. An example outline using the interactive exercise 'Cox' from earlier in this book is as follows.

'Cox' Exercise

Following a complaint from Susan Haddock (a visitor to the hospital), the candidates met Ashley Cox, a hospital painter and decorator. Susan Haddock had heard another painter make offensive comments to Cox. Cox had not retaliated to these comments and, as a result of Susan Haddock's complaint, the candidates met Cox to discuss what took place. The competency areas being assessed were Problem Solving; Community and Customer Focus; Effective Communication; and Respect for Race and Diversity.

You scored as follows:

Problem Solving	Grade A
Community and Customer Focus	Grade D
Effective Communication	Grade B
Respect for Race and Diversity	Grade C

Candidates who scored less strongly tended not to consider the Equality Policy or did not state how they felt about the other painter's behaviour. They also did not ask Cox about his thoughts regarding the situation or possible remedies.

Candidates should reconsider the competency area(s) they scored poorly in – in this case, Community and Customer Focus.

It is not possible to give candidates further detailed feedback as the exercises may still be in use.

Resitting the Assessment Centre

There is a national set time limit before candidates may resit the Assessment Centre. Currently this is six months but, if a candidate is unsuccessful in the competency area Respect for Race and Diversity, it is extended to 12 months. The purpose of these time limits is to give candidates the opportunity to reflect on their performance and on the feedback they have received so that they may develop their skills.

Should a candidate have multiple applications into a number of Police Services the candidate would still only be allowed to sit one Assessment Centre within the prescribed time period. A pass from one Assessment Centre for one Police Service may be accepted by another; however, they would not allow this to be a method of candidates avoiding delays in recruiting.

Using the feedback if you are successful

Following their appointment to a force, candidates are expected to use the feedback they received from the Assessment Centre to identify those competency areas that need developing during their initial training. Guided by their trainers, candidates will draw up action plans for those competency areas they are weak in.

Monitoring the Assessment Centre

The results from the Assessment Centre are constantly monitored, particularly with regard to candidates' sex, race, age and educational attainment. If it becomes apparent that a particular group is being unfairly disadvantaged, research will be undertaken to assess what is happening and why it is happening. Action will then be taken to remedy the situation.

TOP TIPS

- Raise any issues or concerns you may have regarding the Assessment Centre before you leave.

- Complete and return the candidate questionnaire.

- Try to relax for a while when you have completed the Assessment Centre, particularly before driving.

- Find out about and prepare for the fitness test.

- Should there be a second interview, ask the force about its structure and content and prepare accordingly.

- Take time to digest your results and the feedback you receive.

- Use this feedback in your action plans.

INDIVIDUAL LEARNING POINTS

_____

_____

_____

_____

_____

_____

_____

_____

Appendix A
National Core Competencies

Reproduced in part from *The Integrated Competency Behavioural Framework – Version 9.0* (May 2007) by Skills for Justice

1 Competency Area: Respect for Race and Diversity

Considers and shows respect for the opinions, circumstances and feelings of colleagues and members of the public, no matter what their race, religion, position, background, circumstances, status or appearance.

Required level

Understands other people's views and takes them into account. Is tactful and diplomatic when dealing with people. Treats them with dignity and respect at all times. Understands and is sensitive to social, cultural and racial differences.

Positive indicators

- Sees issues from other people's viewpoints.

- Is polite, tolerant and patient with people inside and outside the organisation, treating them with respect and dignity.

- Respects the needs of everyone involved when sorting out disagreements.

- Shows understanding and sensitivity to people's problems and vulnerabilities.

- Deals with diversity issues and gives positive, practical support to staff who may feel vulnerable.

- Listens to and values other's view and opinions.

- Uses language in an appropriate way and is sensitive to the way it may affect people.

- Acknowledges and respects a broad range of social and cultural customs, beliefs and values within the law.

- Understands what offends others and adapts own actions accordingly.

- Respects and maintains confidentiality, wherever appropriate.

- Delivers difficult messages sensitively.

- Challenges inappropriate attitudes, language and behaviour that is abusive, aggressive or discriminatory.

- Takes into account others' personal needs and interests.
- Supports minority groups both inside and outside their organisation.

Negative indicators

- Does not consider other people's feelings.
- Does not encourage people to talk about personal issues.
- Criticises people without considering their feelings and motivation.
- Makes situations worse with inappropriate remarks, language or behaviour.
- Is thoughtless and tactless when dealing with people.
- Is dismissive and impatient with people.
- Does not respect confidentiality.
- Unnecessarily emphasises power and control in situations where this is not appropriate.
- Intimidates others in an aggressive and overpowering way.
- Uses humour inappropriately.
- Shows bias and prejudice when dealing with people.

2 Competency Area: Team Working

Develops strong working relationships inside and outside the team to achieve common goals. Breaks down barriers between groups and involves others in discussions and decisions.

Required level

Works effectively as a team member and helps build relationships within it. Actively helps and supports others to achieve team goals.

Positive indicators

- Understands own role in a team.
- Actively supports and assists the team to reach their objectives.
- Is approachable and friendly to others.
- Makes time to get to know people.
- Co-operates with and supports others.
- Offers to help other people.
- Asks for and accepts help when needed.
- Develops mutual trust and confidence in others.
- Willingly takes on unpopular or routine tasks.
- Contributes to team objectives no matter what the direct personal benefit may be.

- Acknowledges that there is often a need to be a member of more than one team.

- Takes pride in their team and promotes their team's performance to others.

Negative indicators

- Does not volunteer to help other team members.

- Is only interested in taking part in high-profile and interesting activities.

- Takes credit for successes without recognising the contribution of others.

- Works to own agenda rather than contributing to team performance.

- Allows small exclusive groups of people to develop.

- Plays one person off against another.

- Restricts and controls what information is shared.

- Does not let people say what they think.

- Does not offer advice or get advice from others.

- Shows little interest in working jointly with other groups to meet the goals of everyone involved.

- Does not discourage conflict within the organisation.

3 Competency Area: Community and Customer Focus

Focuses on the customer and provides a high-quality service that is tailored to meet their individual needs. Understands the communities that are served and shows an active commitment to policing that reflects their needs and concerns.

Required level

Provides a high level of service to customers. Maintains contact with customers, works out what they need and responds to them.

Positive indicators

- Presents an appropriate image to the public and other organisations.

- Supports strategies that aim to build an organisation that reflects the community it serves.

- Focuses on the customer in all activities.

- Tries to sort out customers' problems as quickly as possible.

- Apologises when they are at fault or have made mistakes.

- Responds quickly to customer requests.

- Makes sure that customers are satisfied with the service they receive.

- Manages customer expectations.

- Keeps customers updated on progress.

- Balances community and organisational interests.

- Sorts out errors or mistakes as quickly as possible.

Negative indicators

- Is not customer focused and does not consider individual needs.

- Does not tell customers what is going on.

- Presents an unprofessional image to customers.

- Only sees a situation from their own view, not from the customer's view.

- Shows little interest in the customer – only deals with their immediate problem.

- Does not respond to the needs of the local community.

- Focuses on organisational issues rather than customer needs.

- Does not make the most of opportunities to talk to people in the community.

- Slow to respond to customers' requests.

- Fails to check that customers' needs have been met.

4 Competency Area: Effective Communication

Communicates ideas and information effectively, both verbally and in writing. Uses language and a style of communication that is appropriate to the situation and people being addressed. Makes sure that others understand what is going on.

Required level

Communicates all needs, instructions and decisions clearly. Adapts the style of communication to meet the needs of the audience. Checks for understanding.

Positive indicators

- Deals with issues directly.

- Clearly communicates needs and instructions.

- Clearly explains management decisions and policy, and the reasons behind them.

- Communicates face to face wherever possible and if it is appropriate.

- Speaks with authority and confidence.

- Changes the style of communication to meet the needs of the audience.

- Manages group discussions effectively.

- Summarises information to check people understand it.

- Supports arguments and recommendations effectively in writing.

- Produces well-structured reports and written summaries.

Negative indicators

- Is hesitant, nervous and uncertain when speaking.

- Speaks without first thinking through what to say.

- Uses inappropriate language or jargon.

- Speaks in a rambling way.

- Does not consider the target audience.

- Avoids answering difficult questions.

- Does not give full information without being questioned.

- Writes in an unstructured way.

- Uses poor spelling, punctuation and grammar.

- Assumes others understand what has been said without actually checking.

- Does not listen, and interrupts at inappropriate times.

5 Competency Area: Problem Solving

Gathers information from a range of sources. Analyses information to identify problems and issues, and makes effective decisions.

Required level

Gathers enough relevant information to understand specific issues and events. Uses information to identify problems and draw logical conclusions. Makes good decisions.

Positive indicators

- Identifies where to get information and gets it.

- Gets as much information as is appropriate on all aspects of a problem.

- Separates relevant information from irrelevant information, and important information from unimportant information.

- Takes in information quickly and accurately.

- Reviews all the information gathered to understand the situation and draw logical conclusions.

- Identifies and links causes and effects.

- Identifies what can and cannot be changed.

- Takes a systematic approach to solving problems.

- Remains impartial and avoids jumping to conclusions.

- Refers to procedures and precedents, as necessary, before making decisions.

- Makes good decisions that take account of all relevant factors.

Negative indicators

- Does not deal with problems in detail and does not identify underlying issues.

- Does not gather enough information before coming to conclusions.

- Does not consult other people who may have extra information.

- Does not research background.

- Shows no interest in gathering or using intelligence.

- Does not gather evidence.

- Makes assumptions about the facts of a situation.

- Does not notice problems until they have become significant issues.

- Gets stuck in the detail of complex situations and cannot see the main issues.

- Reacts without considering all the angles.

- Becomes distracted by minor issues.

6 Competency Area: Personal Responsibility

Takes personal responsibility for making things happen and achieving results. Displays motivation, commitment, perseverance and conscientiousness. Acts with a high degree of integrity.

Required level

Takes personal responsibility for own actions and for sorting out issues or problems that arise. Is focused on achieving results to required standards and developing skills and knowledge.

Positive indicators

- Accepts personal responsibility for own decisions and actions.

- Takes action to resolve problems and fulfil own responsibilities.

- Keeps promises and does not let colleagues down.

- Takes pride in own work.

- Is conscientious in completing work on time.

- Follows things through to a satisfactory conclusion.

- Displays initiative, taking on tasks without having to be asked.

- Self-motivated, showing enthusiasm and dedication to their role.

- Focuses on a task even if it is routine.

- Improves own professional knowledge and keeps it up to date.

- Is open, honest and genuine, standing up for what is right.

- Makes decisions based upon ethical consideration and organisational integrity.

- Aware of their own strengths and weaknesses.

Negative indicators

- Passes responsibility upwards inappropriately.

- Is not concerned about letting others down.

- Will not deal with issues, just hopes that they will go away.

- Blames others rather than admitting to mistakes or looking for help.

- Unwilling to take on responsibility.

- Puts in the minimum effort that is needed to get by.

- Shows a negative and disruptive attitude.

- Shows little energy or enthusiasm for work.

- Expresses a cynical attitude to the organisation and their job.

- Gives up easily when faced with problems.

- Fails to recognise personal weaknesses and development needs.

- Makes little or no attempt to develop self or keep up to date.

7 Competency Area: Resilience

Shows resilience, even in difficult circumstances. Prepared to make difficult decisions and has the confidence to see them through.

Required level

Shows reliability and resilience in difficult circumstances. Remains calm and confident, and responds logically and decisively in difficult situations.

Positive indicators

- Is reliable in a crisis, remains calm and thinks clearly.

- Sorts out conflict and deals with hostility and provocation in a calm and restrained way.

- Responds to challenges rationally, avoiding inappropriate emotion.

- Deals with difficult emotional issues and then moves on.

- Manages conflicting pressures and tensions.

- Maintains professional ethics when confronted with pressure from others.

- Copes with ambiguity and deals with uncertainty and frustration.

- Resists pressure to make quick decisions where full consideration is needed.

- Remains focused and in control of situations.

- Makes and carries through decisions, even if they are unpopular, difficult or controversial.

- Stands firmly by a position when it is right to do so.

- Defends their staff from excessive criticisms from outside the team.

Negative indicators

- Gets easily upset, frustrated and annoyed.

- Panics and becomes agitated when problems arise.

- Walks away from confrontation when it would be more appropriate to get involved.

- Needs constant reassurance, support and supervision.

- Uses inappropriate physical force.

- Gets too emotionally involved in situations.

- Reacts inappropriately when faced with rude or abusive people.

- Deals with situations aggressively.

- Complains and whinges about problems rather than dealing with them.

- Gives in inappropriately when under pressure.

- Worries about making mistakes and avoids difficult situations wherever possible.

Appendix B

National Core Competencies: Checklist

Respect for Race and Diversity

Strengths

Areas for development

Team Working

Strengths

> *Areas for development*

Community and Customer Focus

> *Strengths*

> *Areas for development*

Effective Communication

> *Strengths*

> *Areas for development*

Problem Solving

Strengths

Areas for development

Personal Responsibility

Strengths

Areas for development

Resilience

Strengths

Areas for development

Appendix C
Central Hospital Trust: Information Pack

Central Hospital Trust

Welcome.

We are delighted that you have been appointed as a First Contact Officer in the Central Hospital Trust. We hope you will find the job interesting, challenging and rewarding.

You will be formally introduced to the Trust's policies and procedures through a set training process. However, we have found that new staff have found the enclosed information useful.

We hope this will assist you to settle into your new job and would ask that you take time to read and digest the contents.

The following information is included.

- An overview of the Central Hospital Trust
- First Contact Officer's job description
- Patient Confidentiality Policy
- Equality Policy
- Parking Policy

Central Hospital Trust

Overview of the Central Hospital Trust

What we do

The Central Hospital Trust is proud to provide 24-hour, 365 days a year emergency medical care to the immediate and surrounding area. In addition to the emergency provisions, it provides outpatient appointments, maternity care and planned medical procedures. The Trust also provides for minor local procedures to be completed in GPs' surgeries or at temporarily identified accommodation if demand requires it.

How to get here

The Central Hospital Trust is well catered for in terms of regular bus and train services. In addition to public transport there is parking for 1,500 private cars. Parking provision and enforcement are subcontracted to an independent management company. To assist elderly patients the hospital provides a 'Friends of Central Trust Travel Service'. This is where volunteers provide a free private car service to patients who have no other form of transport.

Other facilities

To support staff and patients, an area of the Trust has been given over for shops to provide food, stationery and other items. There are ten outlets in total, all managed by independent companies. The retail outlets are not only used by the hospital population but also by residents local to the area. They operate between the hours of 8.00 a.m. and 10.00 p.m.

No smoking

The Trust is now no-smoking both inside buildings and anywhere outside within the Trust's boundaries. All staff should enforce this policy by politely asking patients and visitors to stop should they see the policy being broken.

First Contact Officers

First Contact Officers have been placed at entrances to all wards and departments. The staff at these areas are to assist all patient and visitors to resolve any non-medical issues or concerns. The Ward Manager or Matron will deal with all medical issues or concerns, in the first instance.

Refreshments for staff

In addition to the independent food retailers, the hospital provides a subsidised restaurant that operates on a 24-hour basis. This is only available to hospital staff or to the Friends of Central Trust Travel Service.

Central Hospital Trust

First Contact Officer's job description

First Contact Officers work in fixed areas at the entrances to all wards and departments. When appropriate they will visit areas of the hospital, as directed, to deal with non-medical issues and concerns.

Time away from the identified fixed areas should be kept to a minimum, as these are the advertised contact points for patients, visitors and staff.

They report to the First Contact Manager and their duty times will be agreed to ensure cover between 8.00 a.m. and 10.00 p.m.

Their main responsibilities are as follows.

- Act as a point of contact for all non-medical issues concerning patients and visitors.
- Receive, inquire into and resolve any non-medical problems concerning staff, patients and visitors.
- Complete written reports on all matters reported to them.
- Ensure the Patient Confidentiality Policy is adhered to and explained fully to patients and visitors when required. They will also be available to give staff advice on this issue.
- Enforce, as required, the no-smoking policy among staff, patients and visitors.
- Give advice to staff, patients and visitors on the Equality Policy.
- Assist the First Contact Manager in ensuring all Trust policies and procedures are complied with.
- Work with the parking and shop managers regarding security and the provision of services.
- Provide assistance, as required, following the activation of fire or security alarms.

Central Hospital Trust

Patient Confidentiality Policy

This Policy applies to all staff.

A duty of confidence arises when one person discloses information to another, where it is reasonable to expect that information will be held in confidence. This relates to all information about or provided by patients.

The general assumption must always be that information about or provided by patients is confidential and should not be used or disclosed in a form that might identify a patient without his or her consent.

The exception to this is where the patient has been notified on admissions (which is standard practice) that information associated with his or her health care will be shared, as required, within the medical environment for his or her benefit. In these cases, explicit consent is not required.

Prior to admission, patients will be asked to nominate an identified person whom the hospital can update following operations or procedures.

The patient and nominated person will have been advised that, once the hospital has updated the nominated person following the operation or procedure, any further callers to the hospital will be directed to him or her.

The patient and identified person will have agreed in advance as to whom and what information should be disclosed.

Central Hospital Trust

Equality Policy

It is intended that all staff, patients and visitors should follow this Policy. This Policy requires that no one on the hospital premises should receive less favourable treatment or be discriminated against because of:

- gender;
- marital status;
- religion;
- political opinion;
- race;
- sexual orientation;
- disability;
- age;
- gender reassignment;
- nationality.

All Trust employees should note and challenge behaviour that is in breach of this Policy. Should they not be able to do so or should it be considered inappropriate to challenge the behaviour at that time, it should be reported to their Line Manager.

This relates to both employment opportunities and the health services provided by the Trust.

Discrimination includes harassment, which means unwelcome or unwanted behaviour.

Any such behaviour is totally unacceptable.

Anyone who feels they are being treated unfairly or without respect should take action. The following are suggestions, although this is not an exhaustive list:

1 Tell the person to stop (they may not know they are behaving inappropriately).

2 Talk to someone else, a manager or friend. They may be able to offer advice or assistance in seeking a resolution. A First Contact Officer will always be a point of contact and will be independent.

3 Make a formal complaint. This should be made in writing to the First Contact Manager.

The Policy seeks to ensure that legislation and the Trust's Policy are complied with and to ensure that everyone is treated with respect and dignity.

Central Hospital Trust

Parking Policy

Parking in the hospital environment is managed and enforced by an independent management company. This is for staff, patients and visitors' private vehicles.

Staff are able to park free of charge providing vehicles are correctly parked in staff-designated zones and vehicles are displaying the appropriate hospital vehicle passes.

All drivers of private vehicles are required to pay the charges for parking as indicated on the prominently displayed boards at the entrance to each car park.

The only exception to this are the 20-minute zones near to the entrances of each ward that allow for free short-term parking for the 'dropping off' and 'picking up' of patients.

Failure to park correctly or pay appropriate charges can lead to the award of a fixed penalty charge against the driver by the management company, who can subsequently enforce any non-payment as a civil debt.

Appendix D
Frequently Asked Questions

Q1 Will having been a PCSO or a Special Constable help me during the Assessment Centre?

A1 *The assessors will not usually know your background and the only element where it is appropriate to mention it is during the interview section. However, you do not receive any additional credit for your answers being police based. The big advantage of having served as a PCSO or a Special Constable relates to having an understanding of what is required to be a constable and you can therefore be more certain that it is the career for you. Also the skills you have learnt and used during fulfilling those roles should be appropriate to use to their best advantage during the assessment process.*

Q2 Can I apply to more than one police service at any one time?

A2 *No, only one application can be progressed with any police service at any one time.*

Q3 If I have a conviction will I automatically be unable to apply?

A3 *It is obviously better not to have a conviction. A number of crimes will mean automatic rejection from the process. This includes anyone who has received a formal caution in the past five years, committed a violent crime or a public order offence. Minor offences in usual circumstances, for example driving at 38 m.p.h. in a 30 m.p.h. limit, would not prevent the application but all con-victions must be declared when making the application.*

Q4 If I'm not successful in my application how long is it before I can reapply?

A4 *The stage at which you are unsuccessful and the reasons for it may cause the time length to vary. It will be within the range of 6 to 12 months. If you are unsuccessful check with the police service, to which you had made the appli-cation, as to when you can reapply.*

Q5 If I'm successful but fail at the fitness tests will I have to go right back to the begin-ning and start again?

A5 *No, you will be allowed three attempts at the fitness test before having to recommence the whole process.*

Q6 If I have a disability will I automatically be unsuccessful?

A6 *The police comply with the Disability Discrimination Act, therefore each case is judged on its own merits considering whether the disability would prevent an individual from doing the job.*

Q7   If I arrive late for the Assessment Centre will I be allowed to take part?

A7   *While every effort would be made to accommodate late arrivals, for whatever reason they occur, due to the nature of the Assessment Centre once it has commenced it is very difficult to include late arrivals. If there was a vacancy later in the day, or during the recruiting event, then you could well be slotted into it. However, very often you have to wait for the next occasion when that police service holds a further assessment process. Sometimes that can be a very lengthy period.*

Q8   If I'm late will that be scored against me during the Assessment Centre?

A8   *No, not at all.*

Q9   If I behave inappropriately during my time at the Assessment Centre, but not during the actual assessment exercises, could that be counted against me?

A9   *Yes. In effect police officers are never off duty so if inappropriate behaviour is observed then this should be taken into account when deciding on someone's suitability to become a police constable.*

Q10   I've heard that under-represented groups get treated more favourably during the assessment centres to ensure more are recruited.

A10   *This is an urban myth. The Assessment Centre complies completely with equality legislation and indeed monitors all groups to see if any one section of society seems to be getting an advantage (or is disadvantaged) during the Assessment Centre. If any patterns seem to emerge where one particular group seems to be doing generally better or worse than other groups then that is investigated to try and ascertain the cause for any imbalances and if any are found then these are immediately acted on.*

Q11   If I can find out about the actual interactive exercises to be used during the Assessment Centre will that be of assistance to me?

A11   *Never try to find out what exercises are to be used, even if you have a friend who goes through the exercises prior to your attendance. There are two reasons for this, the first being that if it comes out that you attempted to find out about the exercises prior to attending you may well be disqualified.*
   Secondly, where people think they know what the exercises are about they very often fail to deal with the situation with an open mind, often coming to conclusions before asking questions to be able to deal with the situation fully. On nearly all occasions this leads to poorer marks awarded to the candidate. One last point on this: people who believe they have information about actual exercises invariably have information that is wrong.

Q13   If I don't finish any exercises during the Assessment Centre does that mean I will score badly?

A13   *While on occasions coming up with options and solutions to a particular situation may be on a checklist for assessors during the written or interactive exercises, more marks will be available for other things you do, such as outlining the facts as you know them, seeking further information or showing appropriate concern for the people involved and the situation. Similarly* *during the interview don't assume you have scored badly just because you don't feel you have fully answered the question. In the psychometric tests try to give an answer to each question because you can't possibly score if you leave an answer blank.*

Q14　Will what I wear be taken into account?

A14　*No, it should be clean and presentable and make you feel at your best. For these reasons most people wear smart trousers or a skirt with a shirt or blouse. The assessors have been trained not to take dress into account and they are monitored throughout the process to ensure they are only awarding marks for the skills and abilities shown by the candidates.*

Q15　Do I need to write perfect English to be able to pass the written exercise?

A15　*It needs to be adequate to fulfil the requirements of being a constable. The key is to keep the written responses you make simple. Only use words you can spell, keeping sentences short and easy to understand so that the meaning of your work is clear.*

Q16　My writing is poor, so what should I do?

A16　*You can only score if your writing can be read. Although it would slow you down, it may be better to write in a print form. While this may cause you to write less it would be better than writing a long response which can't be read. Whatever the style of writing you use will not affect the scoring of your response provided the content can be measured against the marking guide.*

Q17　If I finish before the end of any of the exercises what should I do?

A17　*If you finish early in the interactive exercises or interview then go back to the beginning and recap what you have previously said. This usually triggers candidates' minds to ask further questions or to enlarge on the previously given answers.*

If you finish early during the psychometric tests then take the time to check firstly that you have given your answer to the correct question: it has been known for candidates who decide to leave one question out, to then go on and put their remaining answers next to the wrong question. If you do leave a question out, and you still have time remaining, go on and answer this before checking all your other answers.

If it is the written exercises, take any time you have left at the end to check your work for content and spellings.

Q18　If I make a mistake during the written exercises what should I do?

A18　*Simply put a line through the mistake and rewrite the word. Assessors will not then mark the mistake.*

Q19　I have dyslexia: will this be taken into account at the Assessment Centre?

A19　*You will be asked prior to attending the Assessment Centre whether you have a physical or learning disability. You will be asked for evidence of this and then an appropriate reasonable adjustment will be made.*

Q20   What should I do if I go into an exercise and realise that I know the role actor or assessor?

A20   *You must carry on as though you do not know them and just deal with the exercise, as you would have done if you had not known the role actor or assessor.*

Q21   Can I use a calculator during the numerical reasoning test?

A21   *No, but rough paper is given to assist you to work out your answers. This is not marked.*

Q22   Will I be allowed to take any memory aids, books, etc, into the Assessment Centre?

A22   *No. You will be provided with a room in which to store any personal items on arrival at the Assessment Centre.*

Q23   Will I be allowed a stopwatch or clock to help me time the exercises?

A23   *You will not be allowed any clock or watch that sounds to indicate the end of exercises, etc. However, there is nothing to stop you monitoring your time with a watch or clock provided it doesn't bleep or make similar noises.*

Q24   I'm told that the Assessment Centre can last up to half a day. Will drinks and food be provided?

A24   *It very much depends on the police service to which you've applied and the facilities available. As a minimum water will be provided to candidates. It would be usual for the service to which you've applied to tell you about access to refreshments when they invite you to the Assessment Centre.*

Index